D1413183

Self-Interviews

JAMES DICKEY

Self-Interviews

Recorded and Edited by
Barbara and James Reiss

LOUISIANA STATE UNIVERSITY PRESS
Baton Rouge

Published by arrangement with Doubleday & Company, Inc.

Louisiana Paperback Edition, 1984

ISBN 0-8071-1141-4

Library of Congress Cataloging in Publication Data

Dickey, James.
  Self-interviews.

  1. Dickey, James—Interviews. 2. Authors, American—
20th century—Interviews. I. Reiss, Barbara. II. Reiss,
James. III. Title.
PS3554.I32Z472   1984   811'.54   83-24416
ISBN 0-8071-1141-4 (pbk.)

"Falling," "The Fiend," "The Night Pool," "Springer Mountain," "The
Heaven of Animals," "The Lifeguard," "The Performance," "Sleeping Out
at Easter" from *Poems 1957–1967*, by James Dickey. Copyright © 1960,
1961, 1962, 1965, 1967 by James Dickey. Reprinted by permission of Wesleyan University Press. "Falling," "The Heaven of Animals," and "The
Lifeguard" were first published in *The New Yorker*.

Parts of this book have appeared, in a somewhat different form, in *Made-
moiselle*.

For Maxine

Contents

Introduction

On the dark green dust jacket of the hardback edition of James Dickey's *Poems 1957–1967* there is a ghostly impression of a man's face camouflaged in the dense foliage. If you do not look closely, you will almost certainly miss this face, which blends so perfectly with its background. It is, of course, the face of the poet. Despite his irrepressible smile visible through the foliage, if you did not know him or know *about* him as a novelist or a public figure, you might guess that James Dickey is a typically shy, anonymous sort of "modern poet," perhaps vaguely gray at the temples and thin to the point of vanishing. You might even venture to say—if you did not know him—"Yes, Dickey is probably like many twentieth century poets who prefer to stay in the background and let their poems speak for themselves." You would never expect a typical "modern poet" to do a book like this.

You might expect Dickey to do what many contemporary poets have done when asked about their lives: either politely demur or reply in the most subtly veiled references, skillfully avoiding biographical fallacies. As for their poetry, contemporary poets have been notoriously reticent about publicly revealing what their poems are "about." Learning to avoid the dreaded intentional fallacy, they have consoled themselves with the thought that what matters is not what they *intended* but what their poems *say*. You might expect Dickey to follow his contemporaries and remember, with pride, probably the most reticent twentieth century poet and arch New Critic of them all, T. S. Eliot, persistently refusing to answer questions about the "meaning" of his poetry.

Obviously this book departs drastically from the quietist tradition of New Criticism and perhaps—if we may make claims for our own creation—signals in a still newer criticism in which the poet's own words about his life and poetry matter, at least as much as any biographer or critic's words about him. In *Self-Interviews* James Dickey emerges from the dense foliage on the dust jacket of his Collected Poems, a thicket which, we believe, has too long camouflaged contemporary writers, and he has openly—courageously—committed himself to certain ways of looking at his life and work. Moreover, his commitment has taken the form of an experiment, possibly a new genre in literary criticism.

What, then, is this new genre?

It is not quite like a typical tape-recorded interview. Although Dickey followed our rough outline and addressed his words to us, we were silent participants in the conversations recorded on these pages. Always starting with and returning to our outline, his thoughts ranged freely, digressively, and revealed a far more intimate view of his mind than would have been possible if we had directed his responses with carefully phrased interviewer's questions. In fact the only interviewer hulking behind these pages is Dickey's questioning mind.

Neither can this book be called an autobiography. From the beginning Dickey did not consider it as such, but he told us that this would be the only work resembling a biography that he would ever authorize. There was something pretentious and *final* about the idea of an autobiography which Dickey would have no part of. Still young and developing, he never wanted to sound as though he had all the answers. The tape recorder provided him with a convenient way of speaking tentatively about important matters related to his art. Again, nothing in this book constitutes the last word from James Dickey who is, after all, in the middle—not at the end—of his career.

This new genre, the tape-recorded self-interview, is a form which preserves the uninterrupted flow of a poet's spoken words about his life and poetry. The limitations of this type of book must be obvious to the reader, so we will not belabor them here. Surely all literary forms have their limits, including the most expertly directed interview and the most fully blown autobiography. But the two main virtues of the self-interview might not be so obvious.

First of all, its informal "talk" is highly conducive to the kind of frankness and honesty which a more cautiously composed book might lack. For example, in a spontaneous burst of speech, Dickey states:

> I think a river is the most beautiful thing in nature. *Any* river. Some are more beautiful than others, but any river is more beautiful than anything else I know.

Now this is a staggering statement, particularly considering that Dickey must have driven over the polluted Potomac on his way to work as Poetry Consultant to the Library of Congress. No doubt if he had remembered the Potomac as he sat composing slowly at his desk, he might have sagaciously omitted this statement from a book. The fact is that, on tape, he did not think of the Potomac—or the Hudson or the Monongahela or even his native Chattahoochee, all polluted. There is a kind of unpremeditated reliability here that perhaps suggests more about Dickey than would a more scrupulously written version of the statement. To be sure, *Self-Interviews* does not peddle the sort of mincing tactfulness which diffuses many literary judgments. But it does present the candid, uncompromising opinions of a man unafraid to speak the truth as he sees it, aloud in the scary marketplace of ideas.

Secondly, it presents a long-needed convenient forum for the poet to say something permanent about his own poetry. You would think that some poets would love to write books about their poetry. As we have pointed out, however, it has not been fashionable for contemporary poets to write about their poems; they leave that for the critics! Nowadays there are three main ways a poet has of respectably saying something about his poems: He may give a poetry reading and preface his reading of poems with brief, personal remarks; of course, after the reading his remarks are lost forever. Or he may carry on a literary correspondence with a friend and hope that his friend keeps his letters for a posthumous collection. Finally, he may write an essay like Poe's "The Philosophy of Composition" or Allen Tate's "Narcissus as Narcissus," making sure that the discussion of his poem is embedded in a discussion of some broader topic or prefaced by profuse apologies; it is considered immodest merely to discuss the poem itself, its composition and possible "meaning." A cool disinterest and an almost completely self-effacing modesty are required of the poet today; this attitude is self-imposed, and in fact is a form of censorship. Which might be one reason why ours is an age of criticism still largely ruled by a cadre of formalist academic critics. The poet has abdicated his role—if in fact he ever assumed it in the past—of making his poems *matter* to his readers.

Happily this is not the case with James Dickey. Rejecting the New Critical notion that poems are autonomous, Dickey says:

> I never have been able to disassociate the poem from the poet, and I hope I never will. I really don't believe in Eliot's theory of autotelic art, in which the poem has nothing to do with the man who wrote it. I think that's the most absolute rubbish!

Dickey's discussions of his poetry may be "subjective" and therefore limited, yet they are presented unabashedly as the words of the "person who happened to create the poems." As such they illuminate the close, tricky relationship that ties the artist to his creation, a relationship we have only begun to understand. As we come to understand this, we will be a little farther from the cold ivory tower in which poems have been viewed as isolated mechanisms and not as the products of human sensibility. Certainly the far-reaching humanizing effects of this kind of book go beyond the scope of this Introduction and might conceivably help bridge the great gap between works of art and human values and events.

Early in 1968 when we conceived the idea for *Self-Interviews*, we realized immediately that its subject would have to be a poet of major standing who was extremely articulate and also bold enough to want to participate in an experiment. Who could be more suitable than James Dickey? We were delighted when he consented to our plan.

Armed with tape recorders and an outline, we appeared at Dickey's spacious home in Leesburg, Virginia, in June 1968. Since this was a particularly busy month for him—he was finishing up his two-year term as Poetry Consultant to the Library of Congress—he told us that he would be able to work with us for only a day or so. After some rather forcefully gentle persuasion on our part, though, he saw that our project would need more than a few hours of his time.

For about a week, between trips to Dickey's archery range and many songs on his many guitars, he submitted to our tape-recording sessions with increasing enthusiasm. At first he appeared uneasy with his newly given freedom of speech. More than once he seemed concerned about whether he sounded boring or immodest and even suggested that we enter into a dialogue with him, which we refused to do. Gradually he "warmed up" to the tape recorder, though, and by the third day was delivering ninety-minute monologues with scarcely a pause; by now he was discovering things about himself that even he had not known. Exhilarated, he stayed up most of the third night working on a poem but met us eagerly the next morning, ready to record.

Recording was usually done in the cool of the mornings in Dickey's living room. From the imposing collection of ceramic owls on the mantelpiece to the hunting bows, guitars, books to be reviewed, and copies of *The Southern Review* on tables, chairs, and two risqué-looking *fin de siècle* chaise longues, this was Dickey's world, the world of his poetry. In this world Thunder, a gentle Australian sheep dog, was thoroughly at home sleeping at Dickey's feet as he sat at the tape recorder. And as he spoke about that remarkable poem, "Falling," we could not forget one painting on the wall, a brilliant blue Chagall-ish watercolor with a French poem painted over it, which he said were the painting and poem of the actual Allegheny stewardess who fell to her death from an airplane.

Sprawled on the rug, we listened, fascinated as this book was "talked." Often Chris or Kevin Dickey, home from school, would join us and stare off into space, possibly learning what they had never known about their father. Or Maxine Dickey—charming, lovely—would make us stop for sandwiches. Large, astride an ottoman, holding the microphone in one hand and toying with his flexible watchband in the other, Dickey would glance at our outline and launch into the serene, wild, and sometimes uproarious self-interviews recorded on these pages.

Nearly half of the interviews are devoted to Dickey's literary career and observations on literary subjects. The first two chapters tell about the young poet's slow self-discovery and then recount what must be considered his meteoric rise to success since his first book of poetry in 1960. In Chapter Three Dickey concludes his narrative and goes on to talk about a variety of literary problems, from the creative process to politics and poetry in the *Saturday Review*. In this chapter he digresses furthest from our outline and perhaps makes best use of the method of the self-interview: this is *all* Dickey; as silent "interviewers," we are least conspicuous here.

The second part of the book records the poet's own words about many of his most important poems. At times speaking of how he came to write a poem, at other times speaking of what he intended in a poem, Dickey had no one systematic way of approaching his work. Neither did he wish to deal with a poem exhaustively in his discussions; as he says of his critical method in his Preface to *Babel to Byzantium*:

> I abjure the full-scale critical performance, the huge exegetical tome that quite literally *uses up* the creative work it purports to discuss and leaves little for the less thorough and professional reader to participate in, the critic having made all possible responses to the work *official*: that is, sanctioned by criticism.

The five chapters are arranged chronologically, in order of Dickey's five books as they appear in *Poems 1957–1967*, and the poems are arranged as they appear in the Collected Poems. Part Two, then, is a kind of *vade mecum* for Dickey's Collected Poems as well as an engrossing self-contained sequence about a poet's relationship with his art. Since Dickey has always considered himself primarily a poet, *Self-Interviews* does not deal with his two books of criticism or his recent novel, *Deliverance*.

For the most part the interviews are printed here almost exactly as Dickey spoke them. However, Dickey and we initially agreed that, in the interests of clarity and "readability" —as opposed to "talkability"—the tapes were not to be considered sacrosanct and certain changes were inevitable. We have taken the liberty of deleting redundancies and insignificant utterances like "I mean," "that sort of thing" and "you know"; Dickey would frequently address a "you know" to us and wait for a nod—or a look of consternation—in return. In a few places we have rephrased sentences and re-organized paragraphs to make them clearer. But in no place did we ever alter the original meaning of Dickey's words. In fact Dickey also did his own editing of the tape transcript, and he always okayed even the most minor emendation or deletion we made. Stylistically this book does not pretend to be Flaubertian prose. But owing to Dickey's keen ear for spoken English, the style is far from dull.

Finally, we hope that *Self-Interviews* will serve scholars, poets, students, and laymen alike in understanding the life and work of a distinguished American poet. We also hope that our book may serve as an inspiration for critics and other writers to pursue this line of criticism. The tape recorder—like TV—is here to stay, and we might as well make use of its fullest potential in literary criticism, especially when the need for this kind of criticism is as great as it is. In a part of the tape not included in the book Dickey speaks of the value of video tapes of poets; his remarks may easily be applied to the audio tapes that make up this book:

> [Once] I just happened to see an old, grainy film print, about fifteen seconds long, of F. Scott Fitzgerald and Hemingway sitting and talking at a table in the South of France. Of course, there was no sound to it, but there they were. I couldn't have been more amazed if it had been Chaucer, or Ben Jonson and Shakespeare at the Mermaid Tavern. And I realized that it's a great thing to be able to have a video tape and make a visual presentation of writers reading from their works. My God, suppose we had something like that of Keats reading the "Ode to a Nightingale"? Wouldn't that be stupendous? You'd crawl on your knees a hundred miles to see that, if you were really interested in Keats—and who isn't? Of course, they didn't have the means to do it then, but we do now. Seems to me it would be folly not to use them.

It seemed to us folly not to do this book.

We owe large debts of gratitude to many people who helped make this book possible. Among these people are: Professors Spiro Peterson, William Pratt, and John Reardon, of the English Department at Miami University, and Mr. Gilbert Seat of the Audio-Visual Department at Miami University—who all provided encouraging suggestions for the betterment of this book. Thanks also go to Norman Mailer for suggesting the title of the book; and to Chris, Kevin, and, especially, Maxine Dickey for their help and gracious hospitality during that busy week in Leesburg. Also, a long, loving pat on the back for Cecilia and Joseph Reiss who did some very crucial baby-sitting that allowed us to work on this book. Finally, thanks to the subject of the book himself, James Dickey, for everything—everything!

Barbara and James Reiss
Oxford, Ohio
August 1970

Self-Interviews

Part One

THE POET IN MID-CAREER

Chapter I

Creative Possibilities

My earliest awareness of poetry at all is so far back in the past that it would be almost impossible to say the very, very earliest. But as nearly as I can remember, it was in high school, when I was going to North Fulton High in Atlanta. I didn't care much about poetry, but a couple of poets interested me very much, especially Byron.

Byron is the first poet whose works I ever bought. They were sad, self-righteous poems about how badly he was treated by women. Also, he seemed to me to epitomize the man who both scorned women and was sought out by them, which I suppose is very adolescent. But I liked it anyway. So I read a biography of Byron called *The Pilgrim of Eternity* by John Drinkwater, and I got especially interested in his incestuous relationship with his half-sister, Augusta Leigh. He was such a terrifically good-looking fellow, too! I compared him to a nineteenth century Robert Taylor. I read all his satires and everything that he wrote. But it never occurred to me that I would ever try to write poetry.

I read Shelley also. I remember reading "The Cloud" as a classroom assignment and thinking, "That really is very pretty! That's a very pretty piece of something-or-other about clouds!" But after that, for the next few years, I never had any interest in poetry. You know, you quote a little poetry to girls, and that turns them on one way or another, supposedly. I thought it might, anyway.

But my main interest was in athletics in high school, and

so I had very little time for poetry; it was just something to make me interesting, and in the process, I got interested. This continued during the short time I was at Clemson. Mainly, though, I got interested in poetry in the Air Force, when I had a great deal of intense activity and then long stretches in which I didn't do anything except keep myself amused. During those long stretches, I had become interested enough to take a number of books of poetry overseas with me, especially Conrad Aiken's *Collected Poems,* which I tremendously enjoyed. They were so melting and beautiful and sad and musical. I also took Louis Untermeyer's *Modern American & British Poets,* a couple thousand pages of poets with lots of biographical information about them.

I never have been able to disassociate the poem from the poet, and I hope I never will. I really don't believe in Eliot's theory of autotelic art, in which the poem has nothing to do with the man who wrote it. I think that's the most absolute rubbish! I'm like Malcolm Lowry—a great, great favorite of mine—who is really interested in the work because it leads him to the man. I think they're absolutely incapable of being disassociated from each other. In other words, I would agree with Malcolm Lowry, who read a Norwegian poet who wrote about the sea, Nordahl Grieg, and went to Norway just to meet him, because he had such strong feelings about coming together with the man who could have written those poems.

Now I have the kind of temperament that won't let me be really, deeply interested in a thing without trying to do it myself. If I like to listen to somebody play the guitar, I want to get one and play it myself to see what I can do. The great joy in my life is to do something that I love but have no particular aptitude for and become at least reasonably good at it. This has always been a constant aspect of my personality. As Sartre says—this is a quotation I like very much—"We're not put on this earth to be demi-gods, but only to improve a little."

I have always been much in love with the idea of improvement. Self-improvement sounds like a coupon that you'd cut from the back of a magazine and send in to find out how to better yourself. But I must say that I apparently have a good deal of that quality in my makeup, because I do like to have the sense that I'm getting better at whatever I do, whether it's playing the guitar, shooting archery, writing poetry, novels, or whatever. It may be an illusion, but it's a necessary illusion, at least to me. I have a horror of backsliding, of not being as good at whatever I'm doing as I was last year.

At any rate, in the Air Force I read a lot of poetry. I was not introduced to it by anybody in my family or any teacher or acquaintance. This has its disadvantages, but it also has one enormous advantage. If you get into poetry in this way, you come to look upon poetry as *your* possession, something that *you* discovered, that belongs to you in a way it could never have belonged to you if it had been forced on you. I've always had the feeling that nobody really understands poetry but me because I came to it of my own free will and by a very devious and sometimes painful route; I feel that it's something I've earned. It hasn't been given to me. It's something that I came to because, I suppose, of what my nature essentially is.

There was never anything in my home life, when I was being raised, to indicate that I might eventually be a writer. But my mother used to quote a few lines of Tennyson, usually having to do with death, and also a good many of Longfellow's. She was the only one in the family who had any interest in these things, and I think they were only in the nature of moral homilies. You know:

> For of all sad words of tongue or pen,
> The saddest are these: "It might have been!"

I don't remember where that comes from. But I know she used to quote from Longfellow's "A Psalm of Life":

> Life is real! Life is earnest!
> And the grave is not its goal . . .

Or Tennyson's lines from *In Memoriam:*

> I hold it true whate'er befall;
> I feel it, when I sorrow most;
> 'Tis better to have loved and lost
> Than never to have loved at all.

Things of that nature.

Then, too, my father and I have always been very close. He's a very gentle person, and he was always reading law books and records of famous cases to me. He had a set of law books of famous cases from the trial of Jesus Christ up to the trial of Fatty Arbuckle. And I expect at one time or another, he read them all to me, or we read them to each other. His great heroes as lawyers were men with an oratorical flair. He was very fond of Clarence Darrow, and we read through the Scopes trial transcripts and also read about Sargent Prentice, a lawyer from Mississippi who very eloquently defended some Mississippi boys on trial for murder in Tennessee. That was perhaps his favorite case. He also used to like the speeches of Robert Ingersoll. And this gave me a liking for words that I might otherwise not have had.

In the early forties I went with a remarkable girl whom I almost married. Her maiden name was Gwendolyn Leege and she went to Bryn Mawr. I met her when I was in the service, and we corresponded all the time I was overseas in the Pacific. She introduced me to some experimental writers and also to something for which I will always be grateful, the Gotham Book Mart in New York City. When I got back from the Pacific, I went to New York to see her, and we visited the Gotham Book Mart. There were all the books I had heard about all those years and had never seen copies of. I had some money and mustering-out pay, so I bought a lot of them and began to read. I had a vague notion then that I might try to write a poem myself one day.

When I first began to write, though, I was very much influenced, stylistically, by other poets, as almost all young poets are. I read a lot of modern poets and decided that my contemporaries were much greater than the poets of the past; to me, poets like Dylan Thomas and George Barker were far more to the point, as well as much greater writers, than Donne and Shakespeare and Milton. Kenneth Patchen was a very great favorite of mine at one time. I think he was the first experimental writer I ever read.

Patchen's attitude, that sort of apocalyptic craziness, that visionary quality, appealed to me enormously. What little of Blake I had read seemed to me to be something like that. But the idea of a man from Niles, Ohio, from the industrial Midwest, being a visionary and a mystical poet in the twentieth century seemed to me to be very strange indeed, if not incredible. And if he felt strongly enough to write these visionary poems, then it seemed to me that I might myself be able to do so. So I was very apocalyptic in the beginning!

I was also very taken with George Barker's style, and I thought he was much, much better than Dylan Thomas. He wrote a very flashy kind of poem with a lot of rhetorical devices; he was always doing things like "rummaging in the bloody cellar of my guts," or comparing the human body to trees and talking about his leaves falling. I thought that was marvelous, marvelous! And he talked about Mars in the beginning of World War II as "the red aorta of war," which I think is just terrible now, but I thought it was wonderful then. I'm very glad that I didn't stay under George Barker's influence any longer than I did. But it did, I think, give me a sense of style, maybe not of *that* style, but of style *per se*.

I never did like Auden especially. I rather admire him now, but I never saw the point of him then. He seemed to me a rather clever, intellectual, journalistic versifier. I did some imitations of Stephen Spender though; I liked him very much. Spender seemed to me really a poet: introverted, sensitive, thin-skinned, aware of everything around him and having an intimate relationship with nature. I thought these qualities were wonderful, and still think they are. Now I don't like Spender's work nearly so well as I did, but I surely did like it a lot then. He had a youthful, idealistic quality that I fancied I had myself. Stylistically, Spender was not very important to me, because his style was not as strongly marked *qua* style as George Barker's or Dylan Thomas's, but he was more an influence on my outlook. He also led me to a much, much greater poet, Rilke, whom he, I think, very largely derives from and has translated very well.

But these things didn't happen in an orderly sequence. I just came upon them through somebody else's telling me about them or discovered them myself. In the beginning I didn't write anything that satisfied me at all. But I could occasionally catch glimmers in my work that I couldn't find in anybody else's. I dared not hope that these were really mine. I thought maybe they were just unconscious echoes of somebody whom I didn't even remember reading, and probably a lot of them were.

Right after the war when I went to Vanderbilt University, I had the advantage of studying under some extremely responsible people who seemed to sense that I might possibly do something as a writer. I didn't study with any nationally known teachers of creative writing or take part in any creative writing workshop. I was still undecided about what I wanted to do, and be. I was not a young boy. I was twenty-three years old when I was a freshman at Vanderbilt.

But I was very lucky, in the first English class I had in summer school of 1946, to have a teacher named William Hunter. He was at that time, I believe, from the University of Georgia, and I understand that he now teaches English at Macalester College in St. Paul, Minnesota. He was a very fine teacher; I could see that, even though I had never had a college English class of any distinction before. For our first writing exercise the little girls, recent high school graduates, were writing themes on "What the American Flag Means to Me" or "My First Day on the Campus of Vanderbilt University" or "What I Did with My Summer Vacation"; I wrote about the invasion of Okinawa. After reading my paper to the class, Hunter called me up after class and told me that Vanderbilt had a tradition of trying to encourage writers. He said, "I think your essay is really very promising, even remarkable. So from now on I'll give the class theme assignments, but you just write whatever you want to write and hand it in." That was marvelously encouraging to me. So I gave him whatever I felt like writing, and some of it was like Kenneth Patchen and some like George Barker. I wrote some poems, a sonnet sequence; I also wrote a critical article and a kind of surrealistic play—Hunter said, "Dickey, that play went right by me!"

I went through college gradually building up a belief in myself as a writer. I didn't really think I was markedly original at all, but I thought I might write some kind of solid, intellectually respectable and, with luck, interesting poems. Then in my sophomore year I had the wife of Monroe Spears for one English class. Mrs. Spears introduced me to her husband,

who was as remarkable an intellectual as I have ever met—
and I've met a lot of them.

He was the finest critical literary intellect that I had encountered up to the time I was in college, and he's by far
the finest I have encountered since. He was something of a
cold, distant man, but his mind was like a laser beam. The
fact that a man of this enormous critical acuteness could devote
himself to literature instead of engineering, medicine or something sanctioned by the scientific orthodoxy in this country,
was inspiring to me. At first I thought he might have been
a failed doctor, that he couldn't possibly devote this much
intelligence to a subject as essentially frivolous as I secretly
believed literature to be. But he was not a failed doctor. He
entered into this of his own free volition and was devoting
the enormous energies of a very penetrating mind to literature.
So that gave me great hope. He said he had very little interest
in writing short stories or poems; his emphasis was essentially
critical.

I thought for a while that mine might be also, but I knew
there was something in the critical discipline that didn't satisfy
me. Let me go back to what I said earlier. I've never been
interested in a subject without wanting to do it myself, not
just talking about poetry and writing critical pronunciamentos
about it but trying to engage in the activity, the thing, itself.
I feel very much as Wordsworth did about this, rather than
as Matthew Arnold did. Wordsworth believed that it's better
to fail honorably as a creative artist than to have limited success
as a commentator on what other artists have done. Arnold
said it's very much better to have good criticism from people
who never could have written very good poetry to begin with.
Arnold is doubtless right, but I still sympathize with Wordsworth. I went ahead and tried to write poetry of my own.

Anyway, Monroe Spears got me interested in the eighteenth
century, his specialty. He also helped me to be much less

apocalyptic, which was probably good at that time, and he introduced into my feverish mind the notions of measure, form, and wit. He had me read an awful lot of eighteenth century works, and I got interested in the idea of writing verse satire and still would like to, except that I don't have the touch. I don't think I've ever said anything in a poem that was at all witty, but at least I admire wit when someone else has it. Wit is a very great tool if you have it. Look at Richard Wilbur and Howard Nemerov.

I think this is the greatest age for verse satire since the eighteenth century. There are many more contemptible things now than ever! Suppose someone had written a great verse satire called "The Johnsonad"! The great virtue of the heroic couplet, or indeed any couplet pattern, is that it is very easy to remember. If you say something in two rhyming lines pertaining to, say, a public figure, people are going to remember it, and it's going to have a great deal of influence and maybe even political power. People are so hungry for satire that Dwight MacDonald will suspend his literary values and write about an amateurish and talentless play like *Macbird* as though it were really literature, simply because of MacDonald's hatred for Johnson. If people are that hungry for political satire, they should surely see the possibilities of a full-scale verse mock epic in heroic couplets with contemporary settings.

So I wrote a lot of couplets, and I still like the couplet. I may return to it someday. But gradually I phased out that part of my explorations and then went back to a more expansive, romantic way of writing. I began to get an idea of some new approaches to poetry. I still liked the visionary idea. I didn't know how visionary I was, but I knew that running through my mind, day and night, were all kinds of odd things. And I thought to myself, as I was walking across the campus of Vanderbilt one day, that such things might have been all that William Blake ever saw, *really*. Someone asked Blake, when he looked at the sun, if he did not see a bright disk about the size of a half crown. He said, "Oh, no, I see a multitude of the heavenly host singing and praising the Lord." Well, if you think about the multitude of the heavenly host and look at the sun, and you really believe that the heavenly host exists, this might be said to be a vision. I don't think anybody can actually see angels. But even if Blake did not actually see angels, he put them in his poems; and I remember thinking that his approach could work to advantage in poetry.

But I think I really began to develop as a poet, as least according to my own particular way of looking at things, when I saw the creative possibilities of the lie. My parents were very much against lying in any form. But I think lying, with luck sublimely, is what the creative man does. You never saw anything like Picasso's women; there's never been a storm at sea such as musicians like Ralph Vaughn Williams "describe." If you look out the window, chances are you will not see those angels Blake writes about. It's an illusion: that is, a lie. Picasso once said something to the effect that art is a lie which makes us see the truth, or which makes truth better than it is. This is very much my feeling. When you see this, then you can act in your own way. And this is what the poet wants to do; this should be his sovereign privilege, because the province of a poem is the poet's, and in it he is God. But it took me an awfully long time to realize this. I was constrained by fact. I thought that if I put into a poem something I hadn't actually experienced or seen, it was in essence lying or cheating and was therefore immoral. When I kicked that straw dummy down the stairs, I began to write stuff that satisfied me.

I remember that Spears was looking at some early poems of mine and said, "Why don't you make the narrator do this, that or the other?"

I said, "Because it didn't happen that way."

And he said, "Well, what difference does that make? It would be so much better if you did it that way." I could see it immediately. So I did it that way, and that's when I began to swing, though it was surely a very small motion in the beginning.

After all, I finally concluded, it's not a question of whether the poet is going to manipulate his language or not; he is. It's a question of the effectiveness and the expressive function of the manipulation and how well it comes across. That idea was the bursting of a dam for me. I could see infinite possibilities for expression in such a conception. If you want to write about an owl who can teach a little blind boy in the woods to see, then you try to imagine how it would be. You know it's not ever going to happen that way. You know it's impossible. But it's like Tertullian's proof of God: I believe it *because* it's impossible. Then you enter into the experience that you have imagined and try to realize it. And that entering and committing-to is what makes writing poetry so damned exciting.

Vanderbilt is a school where you can't be interested in literature without being made aware of the Vanderbilt literary tradition and the great days of the late twenties, the days of the Fugitives and *The Fugitive* magazine and of the manifestoes, such as *I'll Take My Stand,* and of the illustrious literary and political heritage of Vanderbilt and the people who made it so: men like Donald Davidson, who was the only one there when I was there, and Robert Penn Warren, Allen Tate, Andrew Lytle, William Yandell Elliot, and the other people who were associated with the group. I began to read around a good deal in their work.

I read John Crowe Ransom, a poet I think is wonderful but whose main example to me was to say, "Go thou and do otherwise." He's a very learnedly witty, technically good poet, yet his tone—which I love in him—would have been disastrous for me. As witty as he was, he was a little bit intellectual, rueful, ironic, and detached for me. But Randall Jarrell appealed to me the most; he came a little later than they. Next to him, Warren, because of his violence. Allen Tate I liked very much, more as a presence, as a kind of literary figure, than as a poet, although some of his poems I was very fond of.

But Randall Jarrell seemed so much like me. He had sort of the same background. He was more intelligent and well-read than I, but there seemed to be something in the temperament of the writer—I hadn't met him at that time—very much like the part of myself I wanted most to set down on paper. There was a humanistic feeling of compassion and gentleness about him. And it's very odd, because I like Warren too, although he is a desperate, ghoulish, nightmarish kind of writer with a very Swiftian strain of excremental and other repulsive imagery. Warren's hysteria and violence are as powerful as anything in American literature, and I like that immensely. But I felt closer to Jarrell.

At Vanderbilt the dichotomy between industrialism and the predominantly agrarian culture of the South was no longer a burning question, but it was still in the air. So I read an awful lot, mainly of the writings of the Fugitives. I read *I'll Take My Stand,* which is still very powerful, because after all I'm a Southerner too, and the problem pertained to me as it pertained to any other Southerner, or indeed any citizen of the Western world. I read W. J. Cash's *Mind of the South,* which I thought was very good. But the best one of all from my own point of view was *The Attack on Leviathan,* in which Donald Davidson talks about industrialism and its evils and defends regionalism. I had always thought that such an attitude would almost have to be chauvinistic. After all, I thought, I'm not so much a Southerner or an American as a citizen of the world and a human being, which is sort of a nice way to look at it. However, it's not really true.

Davidson points out that you belong to a specific time and place where you can see the same things and a certain number of the same human beings everyday. He says this is far from chauvinistic. This is the way human beings were meant to live. This is the way they can root down into a place and develop their own way of life in harmony with the environment. For Davidson, cultural pluralism is all-important. He says, for example, that when Americans go to Europe, they don't go because it's like America; they want to go there because it's so different, and because there are so many different *kinds of* differences. He says that you can go across a street or a couple of fields and everything changes: the wine, the dress, the food, the music, the mythology. Americans go to Germany because they like the German "thing," or the Munich "thing," which is not the same as the Paris "thing," or the London or the Spanish "thing." I'm really convinced of the truth and the necessity of what Davidson points out: that differences give richness and variety to life and offset the terrible monotony that we're drifting toward in Americanizing the whole world, where eventually there won't be anything but a supermarket culture.

Well, these were important ideas to me, and I began to assess what it really meant for me to be a Southerner. I'm really not quite sure what it does mean in all its implications, but I know it's important. It's important to me to be a Southerner generally in the same way as it's important for a Jew to be a Jew, or whatever else a man might be to be whatever he is. I was born into it—the South—and rather than try to repudiate it, it seems better for me to try to realize the positive benefits there are in the life-situation I grew up in.

Anyway, Vanderbilt had some very positive effects on me. One of them was to make me read a great deal that otherwise I wouldn't have read. I would never have read Coleridge's *Table Talk,* or Hazlitt's essays, or *Don Juan,* or *The Faerie Queene.* (I must say I don't think I'll ever go back to *The Faerie Queene,* but at least I have read it.) I would never have read *The Wealth of Nations,* or *The Decline and Fall of the Roman Empire,* or *Henry Esmond,* or any of the other things I had to read at Vanderbilt. Monroe Spears was a great one for piling on the work. I read two or three novels a week for him, taking elaborate notes. I never would have read *The Confessions of an English Opium Eater.* This is one of the advantages of college; it makes you read so much. That itself is valuable. Taking tests on what you've read has some value perhaps, but the main thing is that you've read it.

I read a great deal of philosophy, especially in aesthetics. That was one of my main subjects at Vanderbilt. (I think it was my minor, or maybe it was my major; I've forgotten.) Also, I took French, Spanish, and some German; I never had taken a foreign language before. I've used them for all they were worth ever since. I also read a lot of psychology and anthropology. For some reason the last two years I was in school I was on an anthropology kick. What especially fascinated me—I didn't know how valuable this was to me until years later—were the people who would go into so-called "primitive" areas and do what would be the equivalent of psychoanalyzing the natives. The difference between the natives' outlook and the outlook of so-called "civilized" people was very instructive to me. W. H. R. River's work was one of the most interesting, as were the works of Malinowski and Radcliffe-Brown.

I also took all the astronomy courses that the university offered. I had a really remarkable teacher in astronomy and astrophysics, Carl Siefert, who was the best teacher I ever had in any subject, with the exception of Monroe Spears. He was first-rate. Through him I got a feeling of intimacy with the cosmos. I had always been like Pascal, frightened by the silence of the infinite spaces, but that was not Siefert's attitude at all. The notion of universal law was very comforting to him. He was not a religious man as far as I knew, but you could tell that every time he discovered another part of the universal mechanism, he was reassured in some strange way. It was not that this made him think about God—I don't know what it made him think about—but he took a very great satisfaction in it. I had never known anybody with any particular attitude toward the universe, but he was always talking about it. He was fond of quoting Edwin Arlington Robinson's line: "The world is a hell of a place, but the universe is a fine thing." My association with him—he was later killed in an automobile accident—was very, very important for me, although I don't think he knew me any better than any of the other students; that really wasn't necessary. My own feeling about it was important. I worked like a demon for Carl Siefert. I had no particular ability in astronomy or any of the complicated mathematics that went with it, but I did my absolute best. And I think I was the high man in the class, oddly enough.

Chapter II

In Medias Res

The most fortunate event of my whole life was my marriage. Without my wife Maxine's encouragement, help, and care of the details that enabled the family to survive, I would never have been able to do what I did. We were married above a feed store in Rossville, Georgia. We weren't even married by the fellow who was supposed to do the wedding ceremony. He was a substitute minister, and we didn't have any witnesses. There's always been a question in my mind about whether we were really married or not. Actually we were, but it wouldn't make any difference to me if we weren't. We knew we were really married only when the government accepted the marriage certificate for the GI Bill.

The first night we were married we went out of Chattanooga down Highway 41 to a dingy little night club to celebrate the nuptials. We didn't know each other very well. We sat there, had a couple of drinks, and started talking about the future. I hadn't given it any thought at all. I was a senior in college; we were married in November. I thought I would try to finish up and then go to graduate school if I could swing it financially. And Maxine said, "Now, I don't want you to pay so much attention to studying all the time. I want you to do your own work." I thought, "Lord, what hath God wrought? That's just what she should have said!" I think my whole career is the direct result of her saying that and taking that attitude about my writing.

She's made possible the whole twenty years since that time,

because I'm naturally a hard worker on my own stuff. To put in a seventeen-hour day writing when I'm really working hard on something is not unusual for me. I don't do that much, thank God, but when I'm really excited about something, especially if I have the prospect of finishing it, then I can write an awfully long time. But I wouldn't have been able to do so much work if I had thought that writing was a self-indulgence that neither myself, my family, nor my economic situation could afford. Maxine created an atmosphere and also a feeling in me that any time I was able to spend on my work was well-spent. That was all I needed, and that's the reason I've written so much.

I was quite a good critic in college; I graduated Magna Cum Laude and was awarded a graduate fellowship—one of the two available at Vanderbilt—mainly on the basis of critical papers. Nobody cared much about what poetry I had written. I published a couple of little things in the student literary magazine, *The Gadfly*. And then when I was a senior, a poem was accepted by the *Sewanee Review* which set me off a bit from the other graduate students. Incidentally, the poem was about my brother's wedding. I have always had very strong family feelings. Maxine (who was working for American Airlines) and I went up for the wedding in Anderson, Indiana, and drove back. We got caught in a great fog and crept along for hours. I wrote about the experience. This was mixed up in my mind—and in the poem—with a trip that my brother and I had made to Florida where we stopped by Marineland and stood and stared in fascination at a huge shark through one of those portholes where you're level with the fish. It was the first shark I'd ever seen that close. All of that somehow got mixed in with my brother's wedding. I sent the poem to John Palmer at the *Sewanee Review*.

Anyhow, I was mainly considered to be a graduate student,

not a poet. The fact that I didn't consider myself completely one of them—that is, *just* a graduate student—was a matter of no concern to the other graduate students or to the graduate faculty. Poetry was just something that *I* was trying to do. It was looked upon as laudable but probably foredoomed.

I was very glad to get my Master's thesis out of the way so that I could find a job teaching Freshman English somewhere, settle down, and try to write. I took a job at Rice University in Houston, Texas. But I was then approaching thirty, and I knew I'd probably be recalled into the Air Force if any kind of emergency came up—which indeed it did. I was recalled and spent two years or so in the Air Force during the Korean War writing very little. During this time my first poem, the one that had been accepted when I was at Vanderbilt, was published in the *Sewanee Review*. That acceptance was one of the things that sustained me during the trauma of being recalled into the service. I had hoped never to be in another plane again. It was a dreadful time for me, as it was for many others. I surely think the Air Force learned its lesson through us, though. It really must have been a nightmare for the regular Air Force personnel, because none of us retreads had any enthusiasm. Everybody just wanted to put his time in and get the hell out. There really was no reason for me to have been recalled. We just sort of stumbled around for several years in the service.

I didn't write much during those years, but by the time I got out of the Air Force and went back to teaching at Rice—Maxine was working at a hillbilly radio station to help us—I was beginning to develop a real working schedule on poems, writing and experimenting a good deal. And I was getting really excited because I sensed some kind of break-through, although nobody would print anything I wrote. I was getting some awfully good letters from editors and very good rejections, with real human handwriting on them—we all know about those.

I was then—this was in '53, I guess—thirty years old, which is relatively late in the game for a lyric poet such as I fancied myself. I felt a sense of entrapment in the academic world at a very low level from which I could not possibly rise without a Ph.D. The Ph.D. was something the people at Rice were insisting on, especially the head of the English Department, Dr. Alan McKillop, who was a very un-understanding person in this regard and whom I have had an extremely strong enmity toward ever since. He didn't *mind* my writing, but he didn't want me around unless I became a reputable scholar. The fact that I had been through two wars, had tried desperately to get educated, and was trying my best to develop as a writer under almost overwhelmingly adverse conditions concerned him not at all.

But I persisted in spite of everything. And then Monroe Spears, who had taken over the editorship of the *Sewanee Review,* accepted a poem and asked if I would like to stand for the second *Sewanee Review* fellowship and send in some more poems. I hastily wrote some and sent them in. And I was elected to the fellowship, so I heard, unanimously. I got a very nice letter from Allen Tate and another from Andrew Lytle, who were editorial advisors and judges of the competition. So I promptly quit Rice—never to return—and went to Europe with my family. There I wrote a good deal and had a few more things published. I then came back to teach at the University of Florida. Andrew Lytle was teaching creative writing at the University of Florida and asked me to come there as his assistant. What I did mainly, though, was not assist him but teach Freshman English as before.

I was then thirty-two and not really doing much. But there was building up in my mind a conviction about how poetry would have to be for me. I had been working with it for a

long time, but I hadn't anything that satisfied me. I didn't
have any sense of personal rhythm that would be recognizable
to me or to anybody else. But I had begun to get some notion
of the kind of poem I wanted to write. I wanted to do something
about sensual experience that had not yet been done. So I
wrote a poem called "The Father's Body" about a child's recognition of the physical differences between himself and his
father. As a result of writing this poem and reading it at the
insistence of a group of ladies at the University of Florida,
I got into a certain amount of trouble which I resolved by
simply walking out. I told Andrew Lytle that I had no further
interest in teaching at the University of Florida—which indeed
I did not, and I haven't seen him to this day—and I told
the authorities there that I had no intention of apologizing for
my supposed transgression. So I left the University and went
to New York to become a businessman of whatever kind it's
possible to become at the age of thirty-three. This was in April
1956. But when I went to New York, I had acceptances in my
pocket from *Poetry* magazine—which had taken "The Father's
Body"—and also from the *Hudson Review*. I had those to sustain me.

I was hired by McCann-Erickson and began to work on the
Coca-Cola account. I did some work on the Eddie Fisher show,
called *Coke Time*. But on weekends I wrote in the hotel room,
the Winslow Hotel—I was known at the advertising agency as
the "Winslow Boy." I had one of those little bitty rooms where
you can stand in the middle and touch all four walls without
raising your arms. By this time I had published a few other
poems in places like the *Beloit Poetry Journal,* and somehow
word that I was in New York had got around to a few interested people, among whom was Oscar Williams, oddly
enough; he treated me very handsomely indeed. At night I went
out with some raffish Bohemian types down in the Village,

editors and poets, some of whom published their own work under pseudonyms. I'll always be grateful to these fellows and ought to record their names here: Bruce Hooton was one, and the other, from Tennessee, was Dave Johnson, who is quite a good poet and publishes under the name of David Gallatin.

I conceived the notion of writing poetry at night and trying my conscientious best to fulfill my advertising commitments in the daytime. Really, if they had told me to say that Coca-Cola was made of green cheese taken from the moon, I would dutifully have written that into every commercial. I think it's absolutely absurd to talk about integrity when you're in something like the advertising business. There's no such thing; it's already a sell-out. The main thing is to be as profitably crooked as you can. It's essentially immoral to say things that people pay you to say. So I had no illusions about being full of integrity as far as the advertising business was concerned; I was in it for the money, to make a living. The integrity came at night, on weekends, at sales meetings, on holidays, or whenever I could get to write my "own thing." After I had been trying to please different people—copy chiefs and assistant creative directors—all day, it was exciting to be able to sit down in front of a typewriter and write something I wanted to. No words could explain how exciting that was: when I could do it my own way! I was selling my soul to the devil all day and trying to buy it back at night.

And so it went for five or six years. I was first in New York, but then I went to Atlanta to work on what's called the local bottler account. Coca-Cola was in the new sizes then, the ten- and twelve-ounce king-size and the big family-size. I worked in that for about three and a half years as senior writer and associate creative director. I had a staff of three or four people working for me, and we worked and worked on that stuff. It was very much like the myth of Sisyphus, pushing the stone up the hill only to have it roll back down.

All during this time I was getting my first book ready. I had a great many loyalties to people in the business world, but the more I wrote and the closer I came to finishing my first book, the more I was drawn away from business and the deeper I was drawn into my own private enterprises. It began to be apparent that under the working conditions of the agency, I wasn't going to be able to give enough time to my own work.

So I left McCann-Erickson and became copy chief for another agency where life went on at a much more leisurely pace. It was a smaller agency, or as they explained it to me, "We have a smaller pie than McCann, but we cut bigger slices for everybody." For about a year and a half I worked on things like Armour Fertilizer and Lay's Potato Chips. I developed some very successful advertising for the new agency, Liller, Neal, Battle and Lindsey; but the more I worked for them the more poetry I wrote, and I saw that I wasn't going to be able to do their work either. By this time, though, I had attracted some attention in the advertising world, and for some reason I was elected Atlanta's "Young Man On the Go" and was very saleable. So I left Liller, Neal, Battle and Lindsey to be creative director for the largest Atlanta-based agency, Burke Dowling Adams, which handles the Delta Airlines account.

By that time *Into the Stone* had come out, *Drowning With Others* was also coming out, and I wanted to make a clean break with the advertising business. I got a Guggenheim Fellowship, and after about six months with Burke Dowling Adams, I quit. I sat down and wrote every day. It was a great joy. I remember the first Monday I didn't have to go to work. It was in August. I took my bow and arrows, got into my old, battered MG, and went out to the archery range. I strung up my bow, stepped down to the first target, and thought, "God Almighty, here I am: where I want to be!"

It seems to me that for commercial purposes business offices cut off a great many potentialities in human beings. You might be a good accountant working for the Coca-Cola Company, but that's *all* you are. That might not be all *you* want to do, but that's all they want to pay you for doing. They don't care what your life is like; *you're* supposed to care about that. But when you spend all your time adding up columns of figures or trying to figure out advertising slogans, you haven't got much heart for the time you're supposed to live like you want to live. Unless you're obsessed with what you're doing in your spare time, you're not going to do very much of it. If you're a poet, you'll be a dilettante poet and write a little bit on weekends, or if you're a painter, you'll be a Sunday painter. In other words, it's going to be a hobby instead of a vocation. And that was above all what I didn't want to happen to me. I didn't want to be known as an advertising executive who dabbled in poetry.

I'm sure this bothered Wallace Stevens too. I don't think anybody in his offices ever knew he wrote poetry until right at the end of his life when he began to get recognition. Maybe he wanted it that way; I don't know. But the notion of a dilettante has never been one that I wanted to apply to me under any circumstances. I've got too much of an obsessive quality about what I do, and I care too much for poetry to be considered a dilettante by other people, but mainly by myself.

While I was at the University of Florida and working in advertising, the poetry I wrote before *Into the Stone* was influenced stylistically not so much by individual writers as by an amalgam of writers: something called, in capital letters, MODERN POETRY. I wanted to make it *sound* like "modern poetry" and not like Stevens or Thomas.

Gradually I began to publish a few things here and there. I remember the first reference to me in print was by a man, I believe named Ashman, in New Orleans. I had published a long, confused poem in *Poetry* magazine called "The First Morning of Cancer." It was a supposedly visionary poem about a man who developed a brain tumor, and dealt with how this would affect his brain chemistry and make him think and see different things. He eventually identified himself with Christ; I don't know exactly how I worked around to that! Mostly it wasn't a very good poem. Anyhow, Ashman was one of the editors of *The New Orleans Poetry Journal*, I think. He wrote that there was a new breed of poets emerging; and some of them were simple, and some of them were complicated, but no one had the right to be as complicated as James Dickey! So be it!

Well, I slowly worked away from the extremely allusive kind of poetry I had been trying to write, doubtless very much under the influence, at several removes, of Pound and Eliot, as well as William Empson, whom I admired a great deal at the time and don't much admire anymore. I began gradually to conceive the notion that it would be better for my particular poetry—based on the kind of person I seem most essentially to be—not to overcomplicate but to simplify down to an extremely individual kind of simplicity. I wanted to find a way to be simple without being thin. This idea evolved over quite a long period of time. I would like to be able to write poetry that would have something for every level of the mind, something that would be accessible to a child and also would give college professors and professional critics something, maybe something they haven't had much of recently, or indeed ever.

I tried to see if I could make effective *statements* in poems, statements that would be arresting and yet syntactically clear and non-allusive, or at least as little allusive as possible, poetry which would be extremely lucid and would at the same time exemplify Alfred North Whitehead's great phrase, "presentational immediacy." I wanted immediacy, the effect of spontaneity, and reader involvement more than anything else. I also wanted to see if I could work with narrative elements in new and maybe peculiar ways. I liked narrative. I liked something that moved from an event or an action through something else, and resolved into something else, so that there was a constant sense of change in the poem; sometimes the change might even be circular and the same at the end as it was at the beginning. I liked to make use of the element of time in a poem instead of having a conventional lyric approach in which a moment of perception, of extreme sensibility, is presented.

Those problems were the most interesting ones to me at the time, and I began to work out solutions to them in verse forms. I worked with the anapest a great deal because I liked it, and because it seems to me to have a carrying flow as well as its well-known hypnotic quality. It has a sound of compellingness about it too, which you don't get in those very prosy organizations like William Carlos Williams'. I have what Richard Wilbur called, speaking of himself, "a thump-loving American ear," and I liked the notion of a basically anapestic norm against which I would then make variations. It seemed to me that in some such fashion I might be able to bring out the musicality of English in ways that nobody had done much of before. So on this premise, and the others that I've just been talking about, I wrote my first book, *Into the Stone*.

In another year I had enough material, writing during office hours, at night, on holidays, weekends, and whenever I could, to make another book which Wesleyan University Press had contracted to publish. On the strength of *Into the Stone* I was given a Guggenheim Fellowship. I think it was six or seven thousand dollars, or maybe it wasn't even that much. I don't remember. But whatever it was, it was fine. It was our escape hatch from the ad business. We were going to leave for Europe in February, but it seemed to me to be dishonest to let the agency I was working for continue under the illusion that I was going to be there permanently, and besides I wanted a few months to work without interruption. So in August of

1961 I left the agency, Burke Dowling Adams, and my wife and I, by devious means, managed to survive financially until February.

The second book, *Drowning With Others,* came out and we went to Europe for nine months, living mainly in Italy. I was writing a good deal. I wrote in *pensiones* and in various hotels. I wrote in Rome; I wrote in Florence; I wrote in Perugia; I wrote in Positano and Naples; I wrote in Munich, in Paris, and in the South of France. Write, write, write. The poems were really flowing.

Most of *Helmets* was written there, and the rest of it was written when I returned and went to Reed College in Oregon as its first writer-in-residence. Some of the poems in *Buckdancer's Choice* I wrote during the latter part of the time I was in Reed and finished in California, where I taught at San Fernando State College, one of those California schools that yesterday was a potato patch and today has twenty thousand students. Two of these poems were also published by a very enterprising young lady at Reed, a senior, in a special gift edition called *Two Poems of the Air,* which came out when we were at Reed. After *Buckdancer's Choice* came out while I was in California, I went to Madison, Wisconsin, for two months as writer-in-residence at the University of Wisconsin. I was there in 1966 when *Buckdancer's Choice* won the National Book Award. I then moved the family from California to Washington, D.C., where I took up the two-year post as Consultant in Poetry to the Library of Congress. My collected poems, *Poems 1957–1967,* came out during this time. I had also been writing criticism from the time I was at the University of Florida, and some of this appeared in two books. The first, published by a small press, was called *The Suspect in Poetry.* Farrar, Straus and Giroux printed a much larger selection called *Babel to Byzantium.* And that brings us to the present, or almost.

Gradually building up through all these years was some kind of career, or pseudo-career, as a public figure giving poetry readings. I gave an awful lot of readings around the country in every imaginable kind of school, under every imaginable kind of circumstance. The result of this I don't really know. The people at the various readings probably should be consulted rather than myself. But for what it's worth from my point of view, although it's exhausting as anything could possibly be to do as much traveling as I've done, it's a very exhilarating and lovely experience. It shows you, among other things, how many good people there are in the world. This is the exhilarating thing, meeting people and being with them in one way or another, people you otherwise would never have known even existed. But the sad thing is that you have such little acquaintance with them, because you're in one day and out the next. You see a face or get interested in a conversation with somebody about Chaucer or Anglo-Saxon at some little school in the Midwest or someplace out in the Pacific Northwest, and you have to terminate it, and it'll probably never be resumed. But it does give you an idea of the infinite possibilities of human relationships, the infinitely large number of combinations of connections with people that are *always* possible under *any* circumstances. And I can't think of this as anything but good.

Chapter III

Teaching, Writing, Reincarnations, and Rivers

Teaching poetry is something that, like most American poets, I've been doing from time to time. I think there's only one justification for any poet teaching, and that is if he thinks he can teach poetry differently from the way it's always been taught because he secretly believes that he has the philosopher's stone of poetry and all the other fellows are dusty academics who don't know what poetry really is. This is an illusion that is absolutely necessary in order to teach poetry at all. And it's one that I've tried very hard to maintain in myself, because I couldn't teach poetry—I wouldn't have the interest or enthusiasm to teach it—if I didn't feel that I was the only one who's ever been privileged to teach it as it really ought to be taught. Teaching is an extremely exciting activity for me. But I have been in and out of teaching for so many years that I can definitely say I have no absolute dependence on it. Only part of my livelihood comes from it. I could make out in any number of other ways. I teach because I believe in it.

The main thing that a teacher can do for a student is what Monroe Spears did for me, confirm the student in his desire to take literature seriously. This is important; in our technology-dominated world the value of literature is getting harder and harder to maintain, but it must be maintained if we're going to have any humanity left at all. The medical profession may save your life, but it can never make your life *worth* saving. It's in the realm of values, the things we set store by, that good teachers of literature operate.

I now teach two main types of courses, although I've taught all kinds, some of them with such abstruse titles as "The Theory and Practice of the Criticism of Poetry from I. A. Richards to W. K. Wimsatt, Jr." But first of all I, and probably most poets, teach workshops in poetry for people who want to write. These are classes in which I try to help students to develop as poets each in his own way. The other type of course is a survey or semi-survey course in modern poetry, which is also quite a lot of fun and makes me read a great deal. What is it Bernard Shaw said somewhere? If you want to learn a subject, teach it? That's exactly right. There's never been more sagacious advice to anybody in the teaching profession.

I remember when I was at Rice, I was assigned to teach a course called "Engineering Composition and Report Writing," a forbidding title—it surely seemed so to me. But to satisfy those engineers and also the requirements of the course, I had to give myself such a thorough grounding in grammar, syntax, spelling, and all the nitty-gritty of writing in English, that I never forgot it. What I know about syntax has not come from teaching courses in literature; it comes from teaching "Engineering Composition and Report Writing." You can learn something from anywhere if you're receptive, if you have what Henry James called "accessibility to experience." So I can tell you whether to use "who" or "whom" in any given context, because I taught "Engineering Composition and Report Writing" at Rice. I know the rules, or at least some of them. You know, engineers go by the rules.

But the exhausting thing for a teaching poet is that if he's really a good teacher, he more than likely will give too much of himself to the teaching and the students, and consequently his energies for his own writing will be diminished. The other extreme is the other kind of teacher—the kind that I dislike most—who considers that his art is sacred and that the attempt of a student to get any of his time is an affront, even an insult, to his self-protective poetic sensibility. It's really no good to say that there should be some compromise between these two types. There just isn't any that works. What we need ideally from a teaching poet is one who has unlimited energy and can give as much to his students as three ordinary men and have more energy for his own work than three ordinary men. But obviously we are subject to the laws of human limitation. He might give and give for a few years, but eventually something is going to have to suffer. Probably the poet's physical condition will suffer. He can't keep giving that much to other people and that much to his own work. It's like Edna St. Vincent Millay's lines about burning the candle at both ends; it *does* give a lovely light, but it *won't* last the night—or it won't last very many years. So there is a sense in which the writer in the university, or anywhere else, has to at least be *somewhat* self-protective. But no completely satisfactory compromise is really possible, ever.

In any case there are two kinds of teaching poets: one whose primary emphasis is on teaching and whose secondary emphasis is on poetry, and another whose emphases are the opposite. As for myself, I'm a writer, and with luck, with very great luck, a poet who incidentally teaches, and not vice-versa. I see a great many of both kinds. Surely university administrations and English departments ought to understand about teaching poets, but mainly it is the poet who must understand what his emotional orientation is going to be. To posit a hypothetical case: if a university administration were to say to the poet, "We think you're devoting yourself entirely too much to your writing and not nearly enough to the students with whom we are paying you to work," he has to be prepared to reply, "My autonomy is not to be violated even by the work that you're paying me to do, and if you're not satisfied with it, I'll move on. But the one thing I will not sacrifice under any circumstances is my relationship to my own work." Now this may sound narcissistic, but the poet, in addition to being more human than other people, is also a fiend and a monster. He's got to have that conviction about his work with which nothing can interfere. He's got to have that absolute certainty that what he's doing is important. No poet has ever been that certain *really,* because the world may not value him as highly as he values himself. But the poet has to say to himself, maybe not "I have important things to say," as Milton says, "that 'the world will not willingly let die,'" but, "Whether or not it means that much to other people or posterity, it means that much to *me.* Therefore, I have got to conduct myself accordingly."

Let me develop this idea for a moment. For every poem published in America, even in a small magazine like *Impetus* or *Kayak,* there must be two or three hundred thousand that never get printed. If a poet takes himself and his work seriously, the labor of writing a poem is almost infinitely difficult. He may be doing it for posterity—probably not; maybe for his friends, maybe for the critics, maybe for some hypothetical public he may eventually have—probably not; mainly he's doing it because he's convinced of the importance of trying to say something using his own psyche, his own life, and his own technical approach and method of saying whatever it is he wants to say. Now this may or may not be important. Certainly commercially it's not very important. But it has something to do with what theologians used to call the soul, or the absolute quintessential being of a person, and it has to do with his attempt to say something about things that have impinged upon his consciousness, things that seem to *him* to be important, whether or not they're important to anybody else.

Now the raw material from which the poet works is memory, which encompasses literally everything that has come to the mind and become consciously or unconsciously assimilated or is in that strange limbo between conscious memory and the un-conscious, where remembered things have what physicists call a half-life. Whatever law operates in the poet's memory to isolate certain information and certain recollections so that they even-tually become poems is not known, and I think, really not knowable. I feel very much as D. H. Lawrence did about this, that it probably is not good to try to be too rational about what are essentially intuitive processes. I have only one rule of thumb about what will eventually wind up as a subject of a poem: something that keeps recurring to me without any apparent reason. In my case at least, the subject which keeps swimming up to the surface of consciousness for no reason has some kind of personal psychic charge. If at that stage I begin to get excited about its formal possibilities as a piece of writing, then I'll probably go ahead and start working on it to see what kind of verbal life it might be capable of having, after a great deal of labor.

Things come together in the memory in the oddest way. I remember that essay of Allen Tate's on his own poem, "Ode to the Confederate Dead," which expressed this as well as anything I ever read on the subject. He talked about how he came to write the "Ode," and the different images and as-sociations the poem had; he spoke about stopping by the gate of a Confederate cemetery, his reading the Eleatic philosophers, Zeno and Parmenides, and so on. Now there's no real reason for Zeno and Parmenides and some of the other associations that are personal to Allen Tate to be in a poem about the Confederate dead, but what the poet and the poem must do is convince the reader that there is some relationship which can be illuminating among these apparently disparate elements. When I read that in Tate's essay, it hit me like a blinding light; that's really what the poetic process is. It's that kind of personal connection of very disparate elements under the fusing heat of the poem's necessity, so that they create the illusion

of belonging together and illuminate each other by providing
an insight by association. It never occurred to me that a poet
could work consciously, or semi-consciously, in this way; so that
Zeno and Parmenides would in fact come to be associated,
at least in this poem, with the Confederate dead and the
effort of the Confederacy. There's a linking-up of the worlds
of the Classical disciplines and the American Civil War in a
way that not only comes to seem plausible but also necessary.
This idea was extremely interesting to me, and it still is. I
don't think Tate or anybody else has realized fully the implications of the idea and what might be done with it if applied
to poetry as a working principle.

I read a lot of Surrealist poetry, but it didn't seem to have
the quality of necessity about it that Tate wanted his poem
to have. It's easy to make bizarre images, like an arrow with
lips of cheese walking across an abyss covered with green moths.
It's sort of fun, and it may lead to something. I think as a
principle it's an interesting tool, but as a panacea for all poetic
ills it's ultimately self-defeating. All sorts of things may be
easily put together in poems. You might put Dean Rusk and
a pair of scissors or an egg beater in the same poem. And if you
called him "the egg beater of American diplomatic policy,"
some people would think that was very funny satire. I don't
think it's funny; good poetry needs something more than that
kind of idling arbitrariness. There's got to be a sense of necessity. But what the sense of necessity is based on varies with
different poems.

Take a good line of poetry, like Shakespeare's "the uncertain glory of an April day," which I think is very beautiful.
The associations of this line are going to be different in detail
for different people, but will be roughly congruent for everybody
in some areas. We all have seen days in April, and we all
know that the weather is very changeable; we all know that the
light of an April day, when the first warm weather is coming

on, is uncertain, but we're glad it's there. I think most of us would have some association of that sort, although my brief "glory of an April day" will take place in Georgia, and yours will take place wherever you remember the April day. Of course the line would mean very little to any of us unless we had seen something we personally associate with it. These personal associations are important; nothing could be more important in poetry. As for Dean Rusk as a pair of scissors or a jungle creeper—now that might be an interesting idea: Vietnam is mostly jungle! "The American jungle creeper"! The incongruity of him, with his bald head and so on, might yield something genuinely good poetically, because areas of association to which more than one person can respond are opened up by it.

I remember reading a review by John Berryman of André Breton, the bellwether of the French Surrealist movement, who had a book published in the forties called *Young Cherry Trees Secured Against Hares.* Berryman said something to the effect that André Breton is a systematic Surrealist, which is to say an *idiot!* I think that's an unnecessarily harsh judgment on Breton, but it probably needed to be said by somebody. Surrealism is not a contemptible device; it's just contemptible as a programmatic sort of procedure that one does more or less as a duty. Some of the Surrealist poets are very fine. Éluard is a fine, fine poet, but only in individual lines. His poems are as formless as anybody else's Surrealist poems, but in fragments the best of them, the love poems, are very beautiful.

Anyhow, I strongly feel that the fabric of memory is probably the only kind of wholeness we have. I think poets value remembered things beyond what most people do, and they cannot bear to believe these things will ever be totally expunged. I read one of the *Journals* of Julian Green a few years ago. He said that the one unforgivable crime the universe has committed against us is that memory can be wiped out, totally destroyed. Years ago I also read something that interested me very much as a poet and a human being. John William Dunne, a mathematician in England, had some curious theories about time. He wrote a strange, rather interesting book called *The New Immortality*. As I remember, his premise was that thought is essentially non-corporeal; the brain is physical, but thought itself is not physical. There's no way to measure any image in your mind; if you see an apple in your mind, it's non-corporeal. And he says that when death occurs, all the thought processes and memories are released from the individual brain into a kind of limbo where they go on making associations forever in endless combinations. I don't know whether I would like that or not. But the poetic process is something like that, *before* death. Combinations of everything available in the thought process from the beginning to the present are part of the process. It may even be *the* process. But I think that the process, though it *works,* is unknowable. There might be some broad, provisional rules under which various kinds of associations could be grouped, but the small, delicate parts of association are not knowable. Maybe they shouldn't be knowable.

I have always believed—and I mean believed *blindly*—in what I choose to call "instinct." I don't know whether the scientist or the philosopher would call it instinct, but I call it instinct. This is one of the reasons why animals have always been so important to me, and especially the instinctual way animals live. A trained athlete, a high jumper or a pole vaulter, will practice and pay attention to his technique; for example, a pole vaulter will practice his approach, run, swing-up, pull-up, his turn over the bar, release, and his drop down into the pit. He will rehearse the technique of pole vaulting many times and consciously pay attention to the equipment and the condition of his body, which has been built up by systematic exercises and tumbling sessions. All of this really builds toward a kind of instinctive act, in which he doesn't think about technique consciously; his motor circuits are grooved by so much practice that he just vaults and does it right.

It's the same with a musical instrument. I used to play the guitar with a very talented and perceptive folk guitarist on the West Coast, Rolf Cahn. He used to talk about instinct in relation to playing the guitar. He said that you play a piece so many times that when you really are able to play well, *you* don't play, you just sit and hold the guitar on your lap, and "the ape plays." That's exactly right. I was playing the guitar at the Library of Congress the other day and didn't have the slightest idea what I was playing. During the playback I went into the recording studio, and the sound was coming over the loudspeaker like there was nothing to it. It's no accident that one of Doc Watson's best and fastest flat-picking pieces is called "Nothing to It." He's doing fabulous things, but it's not hard for him. He just does them. This is an example of consciously working toward an unconscious act.

But animals don't *have* to practice doing a thing over and over again. A bird doesn't practice landing on a telephone wire, consciously watching over each movement of its wings and claws. He doesn't practice like the pole vaulter and the guitarist. For lack of a better term, it comes "naturally" to him. You've never seen a bird miss, either. If a bird wants to land on a telephone wire, he lands on it the first time; or if it's windy and he doesn't, it looks like he intended not to, and he does it the second time. But you rarely see anything in nature that doesn't accomplish exactly what it wants to do. Watch a cat jump onto a table. He might not be able to get there, but this would probably occur only one out of four or five hundred tries. He spends just exactly the amount of energy he needs to get there, and that's *all* he expends; he *flows* up there. Within the limits of their physical capabilities, animals do exactly what they want to do.

Athletes, through their backbreaking training programs, do

approach this state, and that is one of the reasons I'm so interested in them. I read an awfully good essay about the 1924 Olympics by the French writer, Henry de Montherlant. He used to watch the high jumpers warm up. I think the high jump in 1924 was won by an American from the Midwest; I forgot who it was—Ludlow or somebody. His records have all since been surpassed. But Montherlant said he watched all of them jump, and he could tell who was going to win. They were at an easy height—maybe it was 5'10"—and the other jumpers were clearing it by large margins. But Ludlow, or whatever the fellow's name was, was just gradually grazing over the bar at all the low heights as the bar was moved up. Montherlant called Ludlow a superb artist because when he got up to the higher heights where he needed more energy, he wouldn't have expended it worthlessly clearing the low ones by a large margin.

It seems to me that most animals have this superb economy of motion. The instinctual notion of how much energy to expend, the ability to do a thing thoughtlessly and do it right, is a quality that I esteem enormously. I want to get a feeling of this instinctualness into poetry. How to do this linguistically is a difficult thing. That it can or should be done might be an illusion. But it fascinates me to try. For example, I wrote a long poem—I think it's really a failure as a poem, but I would rather have written it than almost any of the others—about a migratory sea bird navigating by instinct. They *do* celestial navigation, you know. Now how could they possibly have been taught that? It's not possible for the mother albatross to tell the little one that if he wants to fly from the North Pole down to the island in the Galápagos, he's got to have a certain constellation three degrees off the starboard wing at such-and-such a latitude, because even *that's* going to change; the angle is going to increase as he goes farther south. But they *do* keep the stars in the right relationship that will get them to this tiny point of land. Now how can that possibly be true? But it *is* true. It is marvelous!

And the time sense of animals is marvelous, not only in migrating birds, but in fish, and in the whole reproductive cycle of certain animals. I don't know whether it's true or not, but I heard something down in Australia about a marsupial wolf in Tasmania that's supposed to be extinct, but occasionally one is seen. I heard that a dead infant was found. But how did the last male and female marsupial wolves in the world ever *find* each other? It might have been by smell or something of that sort, but it might not. Such things fascinate me beyond all measure. The unknowable fascinates me. I don't believe it's possible to know how the albatross or the homing pigeon navigates. I believe that is absolutely beyond comprehension. Apparently it is not subject to the reasoning process, but might short-circuit through it. Again, I don't know.

Maybe I'm talking somewhat out of my depth, but you don't have to know a subject comprehensively for it to excite you as writing material. I think, in some ways, it's better not to know too much about the scientific facts so that you can use them your own way and bring them into your own cosmos. Henry James was once asked—I think he projected writing a novel on the British Army Coldstream Guards—how much research he was going to do, if he was going to live in an army barracks, for example. And he said that all he needed to do to write a novel about the Coldstream Guards was to have one three-minute look through the window of the Officers' Mess.

This approach is especially true of poetry. Now, I don't think John Updike could have written a book about suburban living in Tarbox, Massachusetts, without knowing that kind of life pretty well. But it's very different in the poet's case. It's fine for him to know his subject well; he might write superb poetry out of knowing it well. But he also might write superb poetry out of just knowing it a little bit, having been exposed to it for a second, so that it seems like a vision of something rich and strange, or maybe just strange. In this way the poet has a great advantage over the novelist as far as subject matter and treatment are concerned, because he doesn't *have* to research a thing. He can if he wants to; that might help him. But he doesn't have to; it might hinder him. It's a very delicate matter; sometimes you don't know whether to do it or not.

When I was writing "The Firebombing" I got out my old *P 61 Tech. Manual* and was going to have a long section on different procedures, because flying, especially military flying, is almost all procedure. It was going to be a section right out of the manual about tolerances in the cylinder heads, speeds at which the wheels and flaps were let down, the way the radar equipment worked—all that sort of thing. The section was enormously long and also very boring. Gracious Lord, I would write draft after draft and put in everything that I had in the last draft except little things I would change! (Sometimes I type a sixteen-page poem and do nothing but change a comma, and in the next version put it back in.) But I had all that stuff in "The Firebombing," and then it occurred to me that, to anybody who hadn't flown, it would be very boring. So I made it a more impressionistic version of a combat flight and thought that if I did it this way, it would have greater impact; I'm glad I did; it came out better. These are decisions that poets have to make, at times because of some kind of reasoning process, and at other times because something either feels right or it doesn't.

I believe very much, as Delmore Schwartz said years ago, in the poet writing a great deal and publishing only a comparatively small fragment of what he writes. I've written something every day for twenty years. Most of my days are not days of high inspiration, or *any* inspiration, but just working with the materials themselves seems to me to be important. If a concert pianist doesn't want to practice seven or eight hours, or even one hour a day, I think it's better for him simply to sit and look at the keyboard for five minutes, simply to be in proximity to what he wants to do. Just being in proximity to poems, with the technical problems, the various work sheets, even the pencils and typewriter ribbons—just being *near* poems is important even if you don't write anything or make a revision. Just being there does some good which may not appear immediately but will eventually be of advantage in some way. Who knows how? But I'm convinced that it will. And so I'm always preoccupied with the problems of poetry; I can pick up what I wrote yesterday, and there's nearly always something I can do with it. I may want to change something around, or cast it in a different form, or maybe just put in another comma or take one out. But the main thing is that I'm working steadily with the materials that have to do with my art.

I never have any lay-off periods. And in addition, there are very few hours or even minutes in the day when I'm not turning over some poetic problem in my mind, either the larger aspects of the kind of writing I want to develop, or the smaller details of some specific piece I'm working on, or something I've written a long time ago. The poetic process with me is something that simply goes on all the time, even when I'm sleeping. I write all night when I'm sleeping. It never stops. In dreams most of the time I'm writing, or I'm dreaming about something and trying to write about it at the same time in the dream. And when I'm up, I'm never very far from a notebook; I've always got something to write on. Poetry, instead of being reserved for a special time of the day, goes on continuously.

I don't have beautiful Mozartian flights of the imagination and write down immortal poems without changing a word. That's not the kind of writer I am. I'm one of those slow, plodding, searching writers. I assume tacitly at the beginning of writing a poem that the first fifty ways I try it are all going to be wrong. I work by a painful process of elimination in which, after I've tried every possible way I can think of, I finally get maybe not absolutely the right poem but the poem that is less wrong than the others. As Valéry said, "One never finishes a poem; one abandons it." But I don't think one ought to abandon it without a long and honorable fight to realize it, or to help it realize itself.

As far as the actual writing process is concerned, I'm not really much of a believer in methods of writing poems. Each poem is so different from the others. But to generalize anyway, one almost unfailing constant is that I like to work on things for an awfully long time. Constant experimentation is at the very heart of anything I undertake to do. I look with absolute amazement at the work of poets who just do two or three drafts and then, brother, there it is! That would never occur to me! I would feel I was doing something immoral. It might not be immoral for them, but it would be for me. If I had a pretty good poem on the third draft, I would think, "Boy, this is going to be really good when I have *really* worked on it!" But it would never in the world occur to me to turn loose something with no more labor on it than three drafts. I'm sort of puritanical about this. I believe in expending enormous labors on something to make it as good as I can, to try to get those intuitive flashes of insight to work together in some kind of coherency.

I read an essay not long ago by John Peale Bishop, the poet who was roughly contemporary with the Fugitive group. He said that a really good poet, one who really has the classic virtues, doesn't dissipate his passions in attempting to write poems from which the passion escapes in some kind of emotional expressionism. The poet *builds* the poem so that the passion is conserved and is always available. That's what I want to try to do: not "blow it" in some kind of expressionistic explosion or scatter-shot. I want to try to conserve the passion, wind it up tight like a spring so that it always has that sense of energy and compression, that latency which is always available to anyone who looks for it. I think Bishop is absolutely right.

But then the poet is faced with the problem of means, of finding how to conserve the poem's passion. I think the real poet is going to accept this problem as a challenge, because finding the means is not only one of the most frustrating things in the world; it's also one of the most enjoyable. He asks himself, "Suppose I did this, I wonder what that would do? Suppose I took this line out, or put it down there somewhere? If I change this word, maybe it will work out." The poet enjoys working with the elements themselves just as the painter enjoys working with paints. That's the great fun of it for me. It's not so much that I think I have such terribly important things to say—one hopes that during the process they will develop, or at least be important enough to hold somebody's attention—but as Auden once said, "I like hanging around words listening to what they have to say"; I like trying to see what I can make words do and what kinds of insights different combinations of them will release and make available. When I conceived of an idea that seemed to me to be unusual and interesting, like the one called "A Folk Singer of the Thirties," I thought: "Would it be silly to write a poem about a man during the Depression who is crucified on a boxcar by the railroad police? What if I took that idea seriously? I wonder what would happen."

As Longinus points out, there's a razor's edge between sublimity and absurdity. And that's the edge I try to walk. Sometimes *both* sides are ludicrous! You have to risk people saying, "That's the silliest goddamn thing I ever read!" But I don't think you can get to sublimity without courting the ridiculous. Therefore, a good many of my poems deal with farfetched situations. Wendell Berry, whom I rather like as a poet and critic, read *Helmets* and said that the silliest poem in the book was "Springer Mountain" where an inexperienced hunter tears off his clothes and goes foolishly running after a deer in the woods. Well now, if you want to look at it that way, it *is* silly, I guess. But what's sillier than sexual ecstasy, especially if you're watching somebody else have it? It's not only silly, it's degrading. And yet if you're in the midst of it yourself, it's anything but silly. So much depends not only upon how you look at things, but how capable you are of participating in them. What is sillier than *Hamlet?* It's simply a story about a man who hated his uncle. Yet you wouldn't persuade many literary critics or scholars that it's essentially silly. I think the degree to which you can participate in a play or poem is a very important factor. You have to help the writer, and the poem.

If you insist on literal interpretations of a lot of my poems, of *course* they seem farfetched. They're meant to seem farfetched. My only regret is that I didn't make them more farfetched than I did. Wendell Berry's comments, like many another critic's, give you the impression that we belong to a generation whose catch-word is "Aw, come off it! You don't really feel anything like that." I don't want to come off it! I want to go *with* it! I don't believe in the kind of cool diffidence people nowadays affect, or maybe really have. I think that cynicism is probably the easiest, least profitable, and least valuable human emotion. There's plenty to be cynical about, but cultivating cynicism as a way of life is terribly self-defeating. Lots of writers seem to cultivate it as a literary device, and most of what they turn out is usually very ham-handed and cheap. That's not the way I want to write. Maybe the reason I was never able to be a satirist is that I'm a born believer and not a disbeliever. This doubtless has its dangers. But such as it is, there it is.

There are certain constants in human existence. I think of them as family, love, aging, death, and so on. Now they may not always be constants. The way scientific investigation is progressing, it may be possible eventually to banish death, so that what has been one of the great constants of human existence will no longer obtain. It may be possible to banish disease and halt, or even reverse, the aging process. Eventually science may make it so that *none* of these constants will obtain any longer. But that would be a completely new human condition, and I'm a product, like everybody else, of the *old* human condition in which people *do* get born—that is, of other people instead of by DNA in a test tube—and they do grow up and marry, they do produce their kind, they do age, and they do die. That is the cycle I'm pretty much committed to writing about. And it doesn't make any essential difference whether you die in a prehistoric cave or in a modern hospital full of tubes and antibiotics. The fact you have to face and live through, or maybe die through, is still the fact of dying.

I'm much more interested in a man's relationship to the God-made world, or the universe-made world, than to the man-made world. The natural world seems infinitely more important to me than the man-made world. I remember a statement of D. H. Lawrence's; he said that as a result of our science and industrialization, we have lost the cosmos. The parts of the universe we can investigate by means of machinery and scientific empirical techniques we may understand better than our predecessors did, but we no longer know the universe emotionally. It's a great deal easier to relate to the moon emotionally if the moon figures in a kind of mythology which we have inherited, or maybe invented, than it is to relate to it as a collocation of chemical properties. There's no moon goddess now. But when men believed there was, then the moon was more important, maybe not scientifically, but more important emotionally. It was something a man had a personal relationship to, instead of its being simply a dead stone, a great ruined stone in the sky. The moon has always been very important to me. The astronauts have introduced me to a new kind of mythology about the moon. This may in the end be greater than the old Greek one.

The relationship of the human being to the great natural cycles of birth and death, the seasons, the growing up of plants and the dying of the leaves, the springing up of other plants out of the dead leaves, the generations of animals and of men, all on the heraldic wheel of existence, is very beautiful to me. I don't want to live in a world where the "silent spring" has come. I like to think I'm like Thoreau in this respect. He had a great knowledge—much greater than mine—of the natural world and a great intimacy with it. I don't think knowledge precludes this kind of intimacy. I don't rail against the scientists because they've destroyed the beauty of the rainbow by showing that it's only refracted light shining through the raindrops. It seems to me that we should be able to hold in our minds two things: that it *is* just a refraction of raindrops but that it is also a rainbow, that unearthly, beautiful composition. Which is more important, I think, would depend on the individual.

What I want more than anything else is to have a feeling of wholeness. Specialization has produced some extremely important things, like penicillin and heart transplants. But I don't know how much they compensate for the loss of a sense of intimacy with the natural process. I think you would be very hard-put, for example, to find a more harmonious relationship to an environment than the American Indians had. We can't return to a primitive society; surely this is obvious. But there is a property of the mind which, if encouraged, could have this personally animistic relationship to things.

I go out on the side of a hill, maybe hunting deer, and sit there and see the shadow of night coming over the hill, and I can swear to you there is a part of me that is absolutely untouched by anything civilized. There's a part of me that has never heard of a telephone. By an act of will I can call up the whole past which includes telephones, but there is a half-dreaming, half-animal part of me that is fundamentally primitive. I really believe this, and I try to get it into poems; I don't think this quality should die out of people. It's what gives us a *personal* relationship to the sun and the moon, the flow of rivers, the growth and decay of natural forms, and the cycles of death and rebirth.

Social change is important too. But there are other people, like Norman Mailer, who are much more interested in it and can write about it much better than I can. I would rather sit by a river and watch it. I think a river is the most beautiful thing in nature. *Any* river. Some are more beautiful than others, but any river is more beautiful than anything else I know. It excites me more to write about a river than to write about violence in the streets. And if that's what excites me, by God, that's what I'm going to write about!

I suppose I'm drawn to a philosopher like Heraclitus because of my interest in rivers and the way he uses them as illustrations. He is probably my favorite philosopher because he's so mysterious. You can't *refute* him, because he speaks in parables, in images. "The way up and the way down are the same." The way up to *what*? The way *down* to what? Well, it doesn't matter. What makes it marvelous to me is that it's so evocative. It could apply to anything: it could apply to life; it could apply to the exercise of a craft. I've been trying for years to apply it to my own attempts at writing poetry: "The way up and the way down are the same." The *same*! What does this mean? That the way up to whatever poetic achievement I might be capable of is the way back to my origins, to my first literary style, or what? Who knows? I could go mad pondering such questions, but I also find enormous creative stimulation when I ponder them. And I think this kind of speculation is what the creative person naturally takes to. It's his milieu, his thing. He enjoys speculating, because out of speculation can come, with very great luck, the kind of creative impetus he needs.

This is an era of public pronouncements, and for poetry, too. The other day I read an article in *The Saturday Review* in which a critic urged social commitment on poets. The critic, Judson Jerome—whom I once met at Antioch and thought very highly of—says that poets today must contend with the fact that they are not only dealing with timelessness but are irrevocably bound to the life of their time. Well, fine. But you could reverse that just as easily and say we might be committed to the careening twentieth century, but we are also timeless, and that ought to be remembered, too. One must not be coerced, by Judson Jerome or anybody else, into writing about nothing but temporary events; the larger forms of nature are still there. Not only the Watts and Washington riots exist, but the universe exists as well. Why should we slight *that?* If a man wants to write about the outer reaches of the constellation Scorpio, why should he not be entitled to do it?

Let me develop this idea. There's nothing that says you can't write about the events of your day, and I think if you're genuinely moved by them as a human being and a poet, you should be free to choose what to write about. For example, Yeats writing about the Irish Rebellion and the "troubles" of 1916 has written very great poetry out of events that obtained in Ireland at that time, out of the terrible tragedy and the cross-purposes of those days. The real poet is going to try to make something permanent out of these temporal things, instead of simply throwing the sop of temporality to the public.

Robert Kennedy is being buried on television in the next room as we record this. One cannot help being moved by the spectacle of the people in St. Patrick's Cathedral. But as poets we may or may not want to write about it. The Judson Jeromes would say, perhaps, that it's necessary to write about it. Perhaps Judson Jerome would say that the poet *shouldn't have* the freedom to "cop out," to blink the big issues and outstanding dramatic events of our time. I think he should have the right to cop out. He might want to write about an ant crawling up a leaf. This might be called evasion or lack of commitment. But what guarantees the lifeblood of poetry is simply this: that you are free to write about what entertains your imagination at the time. There's nobody, no law—not even Jerome's Law—that says you *have* to write about any particular event.

I've never read a worse book in my life than *Of Poetry and Power*, a bunch of poets' tributes to John F. Kennedy. They were all *official* poems. Although many poets tried to write tributes to Kennedy, there's not a single poem in the book that's going to survive. *Of Poetry and Power* is the weakest book of poetry that's been published in America in years; there's neither any power in it nor any poetry. It's only official responses, and the official response is the very death of poetry. What poetry has to have is the *un*official response: the response which is crazy, outlandish, cannot be justified by any conceivable public accord. This is what enables Andrew Marvell to walk into a garden and write an immortal poem about it, or to write a poem to his coy mistress—a fine subject, but one never before treated as Marvell treats it. Or John Donne writing about his mistress going to bed. In Victorian England that would have been thought a very improper subject. But these things moved the poets at the time. You can write a great poem on a public occasion, like Tennyson on the death of the Duke of Wellington, a very great poem indeed. But you must *not* be coerced into it. You must not have writers of magazine articles saying that you are "out of it" if you don't write about the Watts and Washington riots and the march on Selma. Public pressure or the pressure of literary groups on poets to write about certain subjects rather than other subjects is the very death of the poetic impulse—partly because it *is* an impulse, not a conditioned reflex.

You must be free to go toward that which genuinely engages your sensibility and craft, otherwise you have nothing but yet another propaganda, a kind of higher propaganda, maybe—though I don't think, from the examples of the anti-Vietnam poems I've read, it's a very high "higher," either. It's just expendable political fodder. There's too much of that in any age. The most high-minded humanitarian sentiments in the world do not suffice to create a good poem. Look at Robert Bly. Robert Bly has no talent at all, but he keeps writing for a pre-tested public, the literary anti-Vietnam public. And when he says something to the effect that Dean Rusk is a bomb waiting to be loaded in a dark hangar, everybody applauds, because this is an anti-Dean Rusk sentiment. Whether or not it's expressed with any kind of poetical, or even human, power is beside the point. The sentiment that one wants to believe is expressed, so everybody applauds. But it's no good as verse; it's absolutely lifeless. The poets who have any kind of commitment to the high calling that they've chosen for themselves will not allow themselves to be stampeded into official propaganda for any cause, no matter how admirable. If you want, propagandize, but *coercion* to propagandize is no good; it will only cause you to write orthodox poetry. Whether it's orthodox poetry in favor of the Victorian world view or in denunciation of the Vietnam War, it is still orthodox, and orthodoxy is the worst enemy of the poet's sensibility and of his freedom to select his own subject by virtue of what moves him as a human being.

One could say that one is a monster *not* to be moved by Vietnam. But monstrousness has always been a part of poetry. It was considered monstrous of Baudelaire to write about the sexual lives of lesbians in Paris. But he wished to do it. He didn't write poems in praise of empires; Victor Hugo did. Baudelaire wrote about the situation between two perverted beings in the depths of Paris, because that was what his emotional makeup caused him to do. One must be free to do this. One must not be coerced. There must be no dictatorship over the sensibility, but a freedom. And it's the *last* freedom!

I think there is a strong relationship between what you write and how you live. If you know, for example, that it's going to help you as a poet to be more observant, you're going to pay more attention to things not much noticed by other people, like the fence around the motel. The ordinary person would notice that it was there, that it was white. He would notice casually a couple of qualities of the fence, but it really wouldn't exist for him completely. But take a novelist like John Updike, who is essentially a poet; he'd take a very vivid interest in that fence. Getting the exact verbal equivalence, as far as he was able, would matter to him. He might have noticed the fence before; he might just be the kind of person who notices things. But for the writer who has a conscious interest in the world because it provides him with the raw material of what he writes, observation has the effect of doubling his interest. He looks at the fence because it interests him and because it's part of the world. He also looks at it from the standpoint of using it as material. So the fact that he's a writer intensifies his interest in the world and his observations. But it also has the obvious effect of making him aware of the world in verbal terms; that is, he does not just notice the fence wordlessly, but notices it through the lens of words and by means of the altering perspective of language. For example, quite a large part of his observance might be that the fence was the shade which is commercially called "eggshell white."

Anyway, the poet's life experience is modified, deepened, intensified because he is a poet and looks at the world in just such a way. The world comes to translate itself continually into highly verbal terms. John Updike and I could look at the fence, and if we wrote forever we would never get the same fence down on paper, because he's looking at it through the lens of his own verbal ingenuity and I'm looking at it through mine. Our views of the world in turn are conditioned by what we are, and what we are is conditioned by the lives we've led as well as different things, like our body chemistry and the degree of acuteness of eyesight or hearing, to say nothing of the enormous associational nimbus that surrounds everything we see and which is placed there by our own psychological processes and memory patterns.

I won't go so far afield in this kind of speculation, because it really belongs more to the realm of aesthetics than to that of the practicing poet. But I will say this: because I dimly and slowly became aware of such considerations, I have drifted into a hard-working hero worship of a few men in literature who represent for me the figure of the totally responsive human being. I think that the further we get into the mechanized world we have created, the more numbing the world is to the sensibilities of most people. It doesn't have to be. A poet like Hart Crane can be terribly excited by machines in a way that he could never have been by the old romantic opera props of poetry such as pastoral scenes, galleons, and sunsets. But I don't think most people are as strongly affected by the mechanized world as Hart Crane. This seems to be one of the reasons that sex and any kind of artificial stimulation, alcohol or drugs or anything else, are becoming more and more important, because we are able to feel less and less in our own selves. Only extremely strong stimuli can have any effect on us anymore.

There are a few men who represent what I would call the "intensified man" or the "totally responsive man." I imagine Shakespeare would represent this for most people. But like anybody else I'm entitled to my private heroes, and my personal heroes of the sensibility are John Keats, James Agee, and Malcolm Lowry.

You cannot read Keats's letters, which I like much better than his poems—in fact, I wish I liked his poems better than I do—without realizing how much everything interested him. There was nothing, not even a fly in the room, that he didn't react to in some way. It's exhausting to participate in one's own existence to such a degree as he did. His doctors were continually telling him he kept himself too nervous. They thought that the tuberculosis, when it first began to show itself, was really the result of a nervous disorder because he lived so intensely and things mattered so much to him. And when he fell in love, that was just too much. His acute sensibility caused those terrible rages and depressions and made him rail at poor Fanny Brawne, who hardly knew what she was getting into; she was an ordinary enough girl. But as Keats says somewhere, he had the kind of nervous temperament that in five minutes magnified the smallest thing into a theme for Sophocles. This has its dangers, and undoubtedly a combination of tuberculosis and this extreme nervous excitement did him in. But such is the writer's part, I think, not only to write but to live like that, in that kind of total responsiveness which is extremely painful but also exalting, and in its best, highest reaches gives one the feeling of omnipotence and infallibility, a great, great feeling. Not many people have that. Keats is one.

James Agee, for me, word by word and sentence by sentence, is the writer I care for more than for anybody I've ever read in any language. It's not only that he was a Southerner and came out of somewhat the same background as I, but that he had the kind of verbal sensibility that my own responds to most. I would agree that his book, *Now Let Us Praise Famous Men*, is exactly what Lionel Trilling said it was, probably the greatest moral document of the time. But to me it's a great deal more than a moral document; it's an example of the ability of the human sensibility to go very deeply into life, not just brush along the surface of it and have nothing left but a few scattered sense impressions. James Agee, for all he drank, and despite the shambles of his emotional life, did have this quality of complete participation, of commitment of the self to whatever it was he contemplated. I think this commitment is tre-

mendously important to a writer. It's because of this that
writers are so unstable. Emotionally at least, a really good poet
is like an engine with the governor off. It's no good for people
to say that life shouldn't mean that much to a poet. By God,
it *does* mean that much, and people will just have to accept it.
The really good poet has no choice; that's the way he is.

The last of the triumvirate is Malcolm Lowry. In a totally
different way from Keats and Agee, Lowry had this extremely deep immersion in things. His attitude appears to me
more comic than either of the others'. There's always some
aspect of whatever he's contemplating that seems amusing to
him, which I rather like. It's kind of a compassionate amusement.

These are men who all died young. All of them have a very
romantic legend about them, and I like that too. But mainly
I like their writing and the particular quality of total response
they were able to get into their writing, Keats especially in
the letters and Agee in *Now Let Us Praise Famous Men*
(well, it's there in anything Agee ever wrote, including those
reviews of old movies that nobody would ordinarily give a
second thought to, if he hadn't written about them); and Lowry
in *Under the Volcano,* some of the short stories from *Hear
Us O Lord in Heaven Thy Dwelling Place,* and the new
volume of letters that came out in 1967. It's there in abundance.

In this connection I would like to make a point I made in
a review of the Greek poet, Nikos Kazantzakis, whom I
think I was a bit overgenerous to as a poet because I wanted
to make a point of my own in the review. The book I reviewed is a continuation of the *Odyssey,* and it's much longer
than the original. I'll quote part of the review, because it
bears on what I'm talking about. I'll just pick up in the middle
of a sentence: ". . . as Odysseus and his followers plunged
through a gorgeously sensuous world which matches the hero's
own tremendous animal vitality as well as his moments of

reflection and turns of his 'many-sided mind.' The feeling of life extravagantly, deeply, and meaningfully lived is in every line of the poem; not only are the personages unforgettably vivid, down to the least slave serving wine in a harbor tavern, but the very objects of the poem seem to have an independent life of their own, too: swords, shields, the robes of the women, the stones on the road, and the stars above the ship all pulsate with uniqueness, mystery, beauty, and immediacy, so that the reader realizes time after time, how very little he himself has been willing to settle for, in living: how much there *is* upon earth: how wild, inexplicable, marvelous, and endless creation is." This is the attitude I have characterized in another place as being essentially life-enhancing. If there's one great gift the poet has to give to humanity, it is just that feeling: that through poetry you are actually enabled to live more, to participate more deeply in your own existence. I don't think anybody could give anybody else a greater gift than that. Even eternal life is not so important, because what is eternal life if you don't have a certain degree of intensity and a feeling of consequence about it?

Incidentally, I don't think heaven would be much fun, from what I've heard. It wouldn't be much fun unless all the worry were taken out of it; surely it wouldn't be much fun if it didn't have this degree of intensity and feeling of consequence about all things. It would be just a void. Robinson Jeffers is a very seriously flawed poet, but he is a poet cast in a large mold. His attitudes are sort of horrifying, but some of the lines in which they are expressed are very beautiful. He says:

> In pleasant ease and security
> How suddenly the soul in a man begins to die.
> He will look up above the stalled oxen
> Envying the cruel falcon,
> And dig under the straw for a stone
> To bruise himself on.

But let me say that I have always been against traditional religion, because my religion has been so personal to *me*. I've always felt that God and I have a very good understanding, and the more that ritualistic services go on, the more God and I stand by and laugh. I don't really believe that the God that created the universe has any interest in the dreadful kind of self-abasement that men go through in religious ceremonies. This may be barbarous to say, but it's exactly the way I feel. God is so much *more* than God. Whatever made this universe, even if it's nothing but blind force, should be worshiped. But whether It acknowledges that worship, or even is aware of it, is very unlikely, in my opinion.

I love the Bible, though. But the Bible to me is a great work of literature only. I know people like Mr. Auden and Mr. Eliot would not agree with me here; such an attitude would cast me in their eyes as a bad man. Remember Auden's lines about people who read the Bible for its prose? Well, I'm one of those people. I don't read the Bible for its holiness at all. Holiness is above and beyond those angels appearing to all those old shepherds every other page of the Old Testament. That's the kind of universe I'd *like* to believe in and live in. But I don't really believe it for a second.

Organized religion, as Eliot keeps pointing out, has as much to do with social cohesion as it has to do with worship. In the sense of being an orthodox Christian, I don't think I've ever been a believer since I was five years old. Church always seemed to me to be very much beside the point. Religion to me involves myself and the universe, and it does not admit of any kind of intermediary, such as Jesus or the Bible. What I *did* like about church was the hymns. I would go to church sometimes with my mother, and I remember consoling myself during all the preachments with the fact that there would eventually be another song. I thought the hymns were great. I still do.

But the religious sense, which seems to me very strong in my work in some weird kind of way, is a very personal kind of stick-and-stone religion. I would have made a great Bushman or an aborigine who believes that spirits inhabit all things. Or that my brother was once a snake, or that I myself was once a turtle. The notion of reincarnation really appeals to me very much. I remember the lines of Ted Roethke talking about coming back after death as an animal of some sort or, "with luck, as a lion." I'd like to be some sort of bird, a migratory sea bird like a tern or a wandering albatross. But until death, until this either happens or doesn't happen, I'll have to keep trying to do it, to die and fly, by words.

Part Two

THE POEM AS SOMETHING
THAT MATTERS

Chapter I

Into the Stone

Let me begin by making one general point. In talking about my poems, I don't want to preclude anybody else's intrepretation. I think it's absolutely essential that everyone should have his own interpretation of my poems, or anybody's poems. I have been asked on this occasion, though, what my poems are supposed to be about from my standpoint, and what I have tried to do in them. But let me emphasize that I'm not trying to impose an official interpretation on the poems; that would be the last thing I would want to do. As one reader of my verse and as the person who happened to create the poems, I offer the following remarks for whatever interest they have to people who want to look at the poems from my standpoint as well as their own.

Into the Stone, my first collection, was brought out by Scribner's *Poets of Today* series and edited by John Hall Wheelock. It was the seventh of eight volumes, in which there were twenty-four poets in all. Generally, I thought, the series was average. But there were some good poets; for example, Louis Simpson, May Swenson, Spencer Brown—whom nobody knows much about but who, I think, is very good—came out in it. However, most of the other poets were not very good and never made much of an impression on the poetical world— if that's important. But I was delighted to be published at all. When my book came out I was thirty-seven, which is late in the day to be publishing a first book of poems.

When I sent the book off to the *Poets of Today* contest,

Wheelock wrote back that the poems should be grouped according to themes; and he suggested a certain order for the poems. I had no notion that that would be of advantage. But it was, because they did group into three or four broad categories: poems about family, poems about war, and poems about love. I think I had a few miscellaneous poems that we just labeled "Others," which seemed to take care of it. As an editor, Wheelock was very encouraging and a great help to me. He was the first one, outside of magazine editors, that I had ever had much to do with. He and Howard Moss are two of the best I've ever had. Howard Moss, the Poetry Editor of *The New Yorker*, in which I was beginning to publish at this time, had been extremely helpful to me. Wheelock and Moss are the kind of editors who say, "Well, as far as I'm concerned, this, that, or the other ought to be done in the poem, but the final decision is with you." Sometimes their advice is very valuable, but I always feel that I could reject what they say without offending them, and I have done so from time to time.

While I was writing *Into the Stone*, I was very much interested in experimenting with verse forms. I've always been a great admirer of Hardy and tried to take a lesson from him in inventing. He seemed to get a good deal of enjoyment from inventing forms. You can look through Hardy's *Collected Poems* and see forms that you never see in any other poets. He has poems which have a very long line—hexameter or even longer than that sometimes—and then a very short line that rhymes with the first one. The physical difference between them is so great you hardly know they rhyme. Hardy's interest in inventing forms is something that I thought I might appropriate, because I have a similar interest. So I invented some new stanza forms. I had some poems in a semi-couplet form, like "The Underground Stream." Another form was based on a relatively simple rhyming quatrain followed by a refrain line. There are a number of these stanzas, and finally their refrain lines make a separate stanza which serves as a summation or coda. I wrote several poems of that sort; the most well-known is "On a Hill Below the Lighthouse." I thought at the time that this was an interesting form, although I now think it's a little gimmicky. The last thing you want to do is to fall in love with your own gimmicks and keep repeating them. So I didn't write any more of those.

There were only a few subjects that I was really interested in writing about at that time. In "The Vegetable King," I try to mythologize my family; this, I guess, is my answer to Eliot's use of the Osiris myth. It was one of the first poems in which I was able to use a myth in a way peculiar to me and at the same time make it something that could happen to anybody. I mention this poem to illustrate that I was working both semi-consciously and quite consciously toward mythologizing my own factual experience. It's not that my experience lent itself more to mythology than anybody else's, but that my own life lent itself to being mythologized just as *much* as anybody else's did.

For example, take the first poem in the collection, "Sleeping Out at Easter." In the spring I *did* sleep out in a sleeping bag in a little pine grove behind my suburban house when I was in the advertising business in Atlanta. But I didn't wake up feeling that I was Christ. That's something I made up. Still, reading the poem again, I feel that I *should* have awakened on Easter thinking I was Christ, in the same sense that every man is Christ and Christ is every man, if you're a believer.

I wrote "Sleeping Out at Easter" in an American business office over a period of two or three weeks. I had been experimenting with these Hardy-like forms: long, long, short, and refrains. But it was always too complicated. The language was too busy, and I was trying to work with a line with a lot of rhetorical effects. It was more of a game than a poem. Randall Jarrell once said of another poet that his lines were so full of effects that reading them was like having one's mouth stuffed with pennies. So I thought, "Now why the hell get so complicated with the line? Nobody wants to read something *that* busy! Why not try to say it starkly, making statements one after the other: this happens, that happens, this happens. And then if you want to become complicated, use an interchangeable refrain technique invented for the occasion." I also told myself, "Make it immediate. Put the reader and yourself *in medias res,* in the middle of an action." So I just sat down and wrote:

> All dark is now no more.
> This forest is drawing a light . . .

I wrote several more lines and thought, "Hot dog! *That* sounds like something!"

Gradually, over a period of several weeks, I worked on it, italicized the refrain, tried a few other things, and it came out the way it is. It seemed to me to be quite a lucid poem— at least more lucid than what I had written up to that time— and at the same time mysterious. On the one hand, the story seems very clear. It's just about a man sleeping in back of his house and becoming another person on Easter through the twin influences of the Easter ritual and of nature itself. His rebirth is symbolized by nothing more or less than waking up in a strange place which is near a familiar place. This seems to me to be obvious, and yet there is here the mysteriousness that I wanted my poems to have:

> My child, mouth open, still sleeping,
> Hears the song in the egg of a bird.

These lines had the marked rhythmical effect I wanted, and also an almost hypnotic beat; perhaps they were almost monotonous, but I hope not too much.

This poem was the beginning of Phase One, I think. I had written and published some poems, but none of them satisfied me like this one. I was under a first-reading contract to *The New Yorker* at this time, so I sent it to them. They thought it was good, but they didn't take it. I thought to myself, "That's all right. Somebody will take this one. This is a good poem." And when *The Virginia Quarterly Review* published it, I was confirmed as one sometimes, or maybe always, desires to be: somebody else thought the same thing. After it was published I decided to write more poems like "Sleeping Out at Easter." I did, but they didn't seem to work out quite like I wanted them to. But I did collect "On the Hill Below the Lighthouse," which uses a similar technique; I still like it. Maybe I like it because it's a good poem, but maybe I also like it because I so fondly remember the incident in the South of France that it was based on.

SLEEPING OUT AT EASTER

All dark is now no more.
This forest is drawing a light.
All Presences change into trees.
One eye opens slowly without me.
My sight is the same as the sun's,
For this is the grave of the king,
Where the earth turns, waking a choir.
    All dark is now no more.

Birds speak, their voices beyond them.
A light has told them their song.
My animal eyes become human
As the Word rises out of the darkness
Where my right hand, buried beneath me,
Hoveringly tingles, with grasping
The source of all song at the root.
    Birds sing, their voices beyond them.

Put down those seeds in your hand.
These trees have not yet been planted.
A light should come round the world,
Yet my army blanket is dark,
That shall sparkle with dew in the sun.
My magical shepherd's cloak
Is not yet alive on my flesh.
    Put down those seeds in your hand.

    In your palm is the secret of waking.
    Unclasp your purple-nailed fingers
    And the wood and the sunlight together
    Shall spring, and make good the world.
    The sounds in the air shall find bodies,
    And a feather shall drift from the pine-top
    You shall feel, with your long-buried hand.
    In your palm is the secret of waking,

For the king's grave turns him to light.
A woman shall look through the window
And see me here, huddled and blazing.
My child, mouth open, still sleeping,
Hears the song in the egg of a bird.
The sun shall have told him that song
Of a father returning from darkness,
    For the king's grave turns you to light.

    All dark is now no more.
    In your palm is the secret of waking.
    Put down those seeds in your hand;
    All Presences change into trees.
    A feather shall drift from the pine-top.
    The sun shall have told you this song,
    For this is the grave of the king;
    For the king's grave turns you to light.

"The String" is another poem with a refrain, written out of my personal experience. I *did* have an older brother, Eugene, who died before I was born, and I *did* gather by implication and hints of family relatives that my mother, an invalid with angina pectoris, would not have dared to have another child if Gene had lived. I was the child who was born as a result of this situation. And I always felt a sense of guilt that my birth depended on my brother's death. Although my mother, a kind and gentle person, would never allow that interpretation to be put on it, that was in fact the case.

We all did string tricks in my family. I actually never heard that my brother did string tricks, but everybody else did. The only way I knew my brother was from a few of his little toys around the house and from a picture of him in a sailor suit that my mother still has on her dresser. A sweet little boy he was, too; he sure looks it. He died from spinal meningitis when he was six years old. But I made him into a child who did string tricks. I can still do lots of them myself, and I taught them to my oldest boy, Chris. It seems to me that the passing-on of the technique of making tricks with string, from the dead through the living brother, who is now a father, to *his* boy, says something about the passing-on of whatever one is privileged to pass on through the generations. And the fact that it's a string seemed to me to be indicative of something important and mysterious that passes between the generations, a kind of thread of continuity.

So I wrote the poem and used the refrain, "Dead before I was born," as a death bell tolling, or something of that sort. I don't know what interpretation other people might put on it. But the obsessive fact in the protagonist's mind is that he had a brother who died before he was born, and his way of communicating with his dead brother is to show . string tricks to his own son.

I've already said something about "The Vegetable King," but let me add that it was an important poem for me because

I tried to take on a larger dimension and get some cultural effects into it. In his notes to *The Waste Land*, Eliot talks about his deliberate use of Near Eastern fertility rituals. A civilization had, in its early stages, a living victim who was torn apart and thrown into the nearest body of water. You can read about this in *The Golden Bough*. The living victim was dismembered, thrown into a river or lake, and was supposed to be gathered together and resurrected when the crops came up in the spring. Eliot talks learnedly about this and about his debt to Frazer. My poem is a small, personal commentary on the same situation Eliot uses for much larger purposes.

As nearly as I can remember, my attitude was that if Eliot used this myth in *The Waste Land*, what if I took an ordinary householder in the spring of the year and, in the same situation as "Sleeping Out at Easter," had him sleep in the backyard and dream that he was the one who was dismembered, thrown into the water, and gathered together again? What if he then came back into the house and realized that this hadn't happened to him except in a dream? But how could he be sure? Maybe when he returned he really *was* the resurrected Vegetable King and the whole spring *had* been brought by him! The flowers on the table and everything else might have been brought about by his death and rebirth, as the people in the Near Eastern cultures believed. I thought, suppose I take this idea seriously and make part of it dream, part reality? Although the man will come back into his house whole, he'll know that next year, with the cycle of the seasons, the same things will happen again. He's again going to be the sacrificial king; he'll be dismembered, but he'll also be resurrected again. The "dread, impending crime" is his own ritual murder, and the "pardon" is his resurrection. Or so I intended, anyway.

I think the most important ability a poet can have is the capacity to commit himself to his own inventions. Not, for example, take the attitude that nobody would believe that a man who lives in the suburbs could be a Vegetable King. This is one of the most important points I've made until now: this absolute belief I have in the poet really *giving* himself to his invention which, with luck, is also his vision. The business of standing back and judging the poem can be done later. But in the process of writing, it's absolutely necessary that he surrender himself and flow with the poem wherever it may go instead of trying to order it in the early stages. So I thought, "It might be crazy for a suburban householder to be a sacrificial god—sacrificial gods haven't been around for quite a long time—but why not? See what will happen."

In retrospect I find that one of the themes in *Into the Stone* is the notion I've always had of a woman as a kind of vision, based upon her inaccessibility. That idea was and still is very important to me, in actuality as well as in poetry. It's important to me—and I assume it's important to other men—that a woman be, as Claudel says, "the promise that cannot be kept." I like to emphasize the "promise" in this, the inaccessibility, the ideal and therefore the intensified desirability of a woman for a man. I have used this concept in many different ways, in the war poem called "The Enclosure" and also in a poem about a sex maniac, "The Fiend."

"The Enclosure" was probably the beginning of this attitude in my poetry. Like "The Performance," it's based on an actual circumstance. On Mindoro during the war, we used to ride in a truck down to the airplanes to fly the missions, and we'd go by a GI hospital. There were a few nurses there, and we would crane over the tailgate and sides of the truck to catch a glimpse of an American girl. We'd occasionally see one walk by, in dungarees: they were unmistakably women. They had the inaccessibility I've always deemed such an important part of the man-woman relationship: the idealization of woman. You can see this idea in many different places, not just in my poems.

Playboy magazine, or any magazine like it, is a perfect example of how men feel. Those pictures contribute, as David Riesman says, to "the enrichment of fantasy."

The poem is based on the paradox that those women were kept under heavy guard, not guarded from the Japanese, but guarded from *me* and the other men who were fighting for them and for other Americans. What I eventually did was simply to take the facts as they were and write about them as vividly as I could: the armed guards and the barbed wire fences that were designed to keep me and my companions from these priceless women, who were really just ordinary American women. The man-woman relationship which had been kept in abeyance for so long would become so intensified that when the war was over and the soldier moved on to occupation duty, he would have an enormous residue of physical passion, fantasy, and yes, love, and he would give it to the enemy's women, who would be available, again paradoxically, as his own countrywomen had never been, during the war.

Almost every word of "The Performance" is literally true, except that the interpretation of the facts is my own. It's a poem about a boy named Donald Armstrong, who came from somewhere in the West. He was in my squadron, the 418th Night Fighter Squadron, during the Second World War. He was probably my best friend in the squadron, a very lovable, ugly fellow. You need somebody like him in a combat situation, someone who sees the humorous side of everything and is happy-go-lucky and daring. He was an awfully good pilot, but he took a lot of unnecessary chances, and the older air crews in the squadron were a bit chary of him. He was always doing crazy things like going to sleep with the airplane on Automatic Pilot. He and his observer—the P61 had a two-man crew—sometimes would both go to sleep and just drone along, coming back from convoy cover or wherever they'd been.

Most of our missions were to the north of the island we were on, Mindoro, the island immediately south of Luzon. But we also had missions to the south, to Panay. As nearly as I can remember, some Japanese held the island and were using Filipino labor to build an airstrip. Armstrong and his observer, Jim Lalley, went down to Panay in a P61 one evening on a strafing run. Apparently it was just at dusk, when it's hard to judge distances, and the plane hit the ground. It was damaged and began to come apart, so Armstrong made a crash landing. They were both hurt, according to the reports we got from the Filipino guerrillas, but they were alive. They were taken out of the aircraft by the Japanese, kept in an old schoolhouse, and beheaded the next day at dawn. We found out about this immediately from the guerrilla forces on Panay, but there was nothing we could have done about it.

Don Armstrong was always doing gymnastic tricks in the squadron area. He used to do flips and all kinds of such things, and would work on his handstands. He was a tall fellow, and because his center of gravity was high, it was hard for him to do handstands. I can remember him falling over on his head and back and getting up and trying again. For a long time I tried to write this poem, but the poems I wrote were all official tributes to my old buddy. They didn't have the distinctiveness that I thought the poem really ought to have. So I said to myself, "Goodness, Jim, what is the thing you remember *most* about Don? Do you remember how ugly he was, or how skinny he was, or something that he did?" There was a squadron movie area where we used to have movies when the Japanese weren't bombing us. Don and I saw a movie called *Laura* there, and he was wild about it. I remember sitting in the weeds watching that movie with him; so I put that into the poem, but it wasn't right. Then I remembered that he used to do all those flips and tricks in the squadron area. People would stand around watching him, but sometimes he'd just be out there by himself standing on his hands, or trying to. He never mastered it; I never saw him do a good handstand.

Finally I tried to bring together the unsuccessful handstand, the last trick he was trying to perfect, and the grotesque manner of his death, and I tried to describe the effect these would have on the beholders, the executioners, and on the poet who tells the poem. I thought, "Why not make it *really* crazy?" The poem isn't about the facts of Armstrong's death, because the narrator is trying to imagine them. I said to myself, "I'll bet that damned Armstrong would be crazy enough to throw off a dozen cartwheels before he got his head chopped off! And what would *that* do to the Japanese?"

Since you can make anything you like happen in a poem, I made it happen that way. I wrote the poem in a rather matter-of-fact way with no obvious rhetorical devices, like refrains. I did it straight because I didn't want to write amazingly about ordinary events, but matter-of-factly about extraordinary events. It seemed to be more effective that way, as well as much truer to the kind of experience that it might have been for the narrator. I suppose "The Performance" is the most anthologized of my poems. I've never taken an actual count, but I've come across it in more places than I have any other of my poems, maybe partly because it's been in circulation longer. I wrote it in the first part of 1958, also in an advertising office.

I'm always trying to synthesize, and I thought, "Boy, next week I'm going to try to get these two techniques together. (I had to drop poetry and do some radio commercials.) I'm going to use the crazy approach to subject matter I used in 'The Performance' and some other things, like refrains, and see what happens." As I said, experimentation is very, very important to me. That's what makes poetry so damned much fun! If you ask yourself the fundamental question, "What would happen if . . . ?" then the only one thing to do is to see what *would* happen if you did such-and-such a thing. That's always been very much a part of writing poetry for me, and that's the part I enjoy the most.

THE PERFORMANCE

The last time I saw Donald Armstrong
He was staggering oddly off into the sun,
Going down, of the Philippine Islands.
I let my shovel fall, and put that hand
Above my eyes, and moved some way to one side
That his body might pass through the sun,

And I saw how well he was not
Standing there on his hands,
On his spindle-shanked forearms balanced,
Unbalanced, with his big feet looming and waving
In the great, untrustworthy air
He flew in each night, when it darkened.

Dust fanned in scraped puffs from the earth
Between his arms, and blood turned his face inside out,
To demonstrate its suppleness
Of veins, as he perfected his role.
Next day, he toppled his head off
On an island beach to the south,

And the enemy's two-handed sword
Did not fall from anyone's hands
At that miraculous sight,
As the head rolled over upon
Its wide-eyed face, and fell
Into the inadequate grave

He had dug for himself, under pressure.
Yet I put my flat hand to my eyebrows
Months later, to see him again
In the sun, when I learned how he died,
And imagined him, there,
Come, judged, before his small captors,

Doing all his lean tricks to amaze them—
The back somersault, the kip-up—
And at last, the stand on his hands,
Perfect, with his feet together,
His head down, evenly breathing,
As the sun poured up from the sea

And the headsman broke down
In a blaze of tears, in that light
Of the thin, long human frame
Upside down in its own strange joy,
And, if some other one had not told him,
Would have cut off the feet

Instead of the head,
And if Armstrong had not presently risen
In kingly, round-shouldered attendance,
And then knelt down in himself
Beside his hacked, glittering grave, having done
All things in this life that he could.

"Walking on Water" is a poem based on the fact that I once saw a little boy who seemed to be standing on the water of Hampton River, in south Georgia. If a little boy stands on a big enough plank, his weight will make it sink under the water just enough to be invisible. The sun shines on the water where he's standing as it shines on any other part of the water. He's actually standing on the plank, but, by God, the illusion is absolutely uncanny! He has a pole and when he poles himself along, it looks like he's just sliding along on the water. He's not actually walking, he's sliding on water, but it's the nearest thing that people have to being able to walk on water. I try to cover that up by saying, "Except for the wrong step of sliding." That's what it looks like. His feet are on top of the water and he's in motion.

Again you *imagine* the situation. I started out with the image of the boy standing on the plank and poling himself from one shore to another. I thought, "Well, let's take this seriously as a miracle." It's kind of a natural miracle. It can be explained, but it looks nonetheless miraculous to the beholder, and so it probably seems miraculous to the person doing it too, and maybe even to the birds and the sharks and fish around him. He would seem to be like a junior Christ. And the shark would follow like a dog, a dangerous brute in a world he never bargained for.

"Awaiting the Swimmer" is a poem that was very exciting to me because I thought I had found an interesting way to talk about cowardice: what it must be like for a man to be in love with a woman like a Hemingwayesque man, in that she's trying to prove something to herself physically; in this case, that she can swim across a river. But the man can't swim; he just stands on the bank with a towel, giving her a point to swim toward. She's the strong-willed one; he's just an adjunct of her, and yet he has to take the male role in love-making. What would this do to their relationship? How would he feel about it? Not how would she feel, but how would *he* feel? I asked myself these questions and proceeded to use the anapest that I was so enamored of in those days. I ended the poem on a question:

> How hope to bear up, when she gives me
> The fear-killing moves of her body?

Because, even thought she might have killed her fears when she swam across the river, his are still quite intact. She might have fulfilled herself, but she's become a frightful presence to him. She's got the whole world's strength that she's taken from it, and he doesn't have anything except uncertainty.

"On the Hill Below the Lighthouse" is a pleasant enough poem. I think there are some nice kinesthetic effects in the description of the shadows moving around the walls as the lighthouse light swings around. Something like this actually does happen; it's something you can observe for yourself next time you're sleeping on the hill below the lighthouse with somebody you love.

When I wrote "Into the Stone," I didn't have any particular person or incident in mind. As nearly as I can remember, I started writing the poem with a vague idea about the quality of a love relationship, especially in its early stages when it changes the world for the person in love. I began with an abstract theory about experience, and especially about love. And gradually I worked out a scheme in which the protagonist goes toward the love object, the woman. Eventually the poem became an assertion that not only the world of the person in love is changed by the new love relationship, but the whole universe is changed. Things happen that never happened before; the moon in the sky turns around and shines with the other side facing the earth. The protagonist doesn't care if this actually happens or not, but the moonlight surely is different and it might very well have come from the moon's dark unknown side, as far as he's concerned. Everything is miraculous, strange, and exciting. This is another poem that has in it a number of relationships that are certainly not defensible logically. It's very much a matter of how one feels: the universe becomes both more intimate and stranger. And the protagonist feels that through being in love he has really come to a self much different from his usual self, one which has the quality of being miraculous and of making the moon, the air, and everything else around him unheard-of and miraculous.

But as for autobiographical considerations, I don't truthfully remember how the poem was written or why it was written.

It was not based on anything that happened to me or on the way I had felt at any time. It was something that I more or less aspired to rather than being the product of something I had actually experienced. I think that, in quite a lot of poems, I write about something I would *hope* to have happen with that degree of intensity, rather than something that *has* happened.

When *Into the Stone* came out, I had no idea what its reception would be. I knew that the *Poets of Today* series had been much reviewed in the first volumes, but I was in Volume Seven. People were getting tired of the Series by that time. In Scribner's large, economy-size package of three first-books in one, I was published along with Paris Leary and Jon Swan, two very uneasy bedfellows indeed. So I didn't expect to get much attention. But there were some reviews which were *extremely* kind. They didn't care much about Paris Leary or Jon Swan, and neither did I. I liked Swan somewhat, but I didn't care much for Paris Leary. James Wright wrote to me about the book, as did some other poets; and it began to seem that it had been worth doing, though I still had many doubts about it, as any poet has about his own work.

But when a first book comes out and you hold it in your hand and read through it, it isn't just the *book* you're thinking about. There I was, thirty-seven years old, asking myself, "What am I going to do now?" The question came to me with a great deal more poignancy than it would have at the age of twenty-three. I thought, "I've taken a modest step up on Parnassus, but quite a lot depends on what I do now. Am I going to write more poems like these, or am I going to consider these poems a platform from which to jump toward another kind of poem?" I didn't want to be known as an occasional poet who just writes poems whenever the mood strikes him. I wanted to be a poet with strongly marked themes so that people could connect the poems with each other, although, hopefully the poems would also be experienced individually. So I sat down and listed about eighty or ninety subjects for poems that I had stored up in notebooks, and I tried to attach some priority to them, which ones I thought were going to be best and which ones I was most excited about writing. And the number-one poem was about Dover, about kingship and its relationship to a person who's been raised in a democracy.

Most American boys have read about kings, but a king to an American is both less and more than he is to an Englishman who lives in a land that traditionally has kings. I thought it might be an extremely complex and interesting problem to write a relatively long poem using all the cliches about kings, about their being confined in dungeons and escaping, about the man in the iron mask, and so on. I decided to work these ideas into a poem about an American tourist and his pregnant wife who land in Dover. The tourist would land in the king country and have a fantasy about being the king and his own unborn son's being the prince. I knew this poem was going to take a long time to write, and I was very anxious to work on it. I wanted to have a refrain, so I thought, "Why don't I have a two-line refrain with the key words changing in those two lines, followed by a one-line refrain, and then interchange the two refrains in various ways?" That seemed ingenious to me, and so I started to work on it. And after about a year and a half, I finally finished, to my satisfaction, a poem called "Dover: Believing in Kings."

Chapter II

Drowning With Others

The book, *Drowning With Others*, was written in American business offices. I would like to believe, because of an example of this kind, that American poets can indulge in a kind of inspired thievery from business houses in America. Business houses are very lucky to get poets. A talented poet can write better advertising copy in five minutes than fifty tired hacks of the advertising business can do in fifty years. But the trouble with poets in advertising is that they can become too successful and reach a point beyond which they are not able to function as poets. And then they will say, "Well, what's the use? Poetry cuts down on my efficiency as a businessman, so it will have to be phased out." I was one who went the other way. Poetry was more important to me than being a successful businessman. Business was an interim stop for me in order to be able to write poetry. *Drowning With Others* was written under the traumatic and blood-letting kinds of circumstances in which you're expected to be working full-time for the business, but you're actually doing "your own thing" part of the time. This makes you feel guilty. But when I finished a poem like "The Lifeguard," I was quite sure that it was a great deal better to have written it than to have worked on the fertilizer copy I was supposed to write at the time. With this conviction, it was obvious to me that eventually I would leave the advertising business.

Anyway, "The Lifeguard" was written in the offices of Liller, Neal, Battle and Lindsey. They were very good people and still remain close friends of mine, but there is a point at which one's artistic integrity depends upon the writing of one particular poem. I felt very much this way about "The Lifeguard," and I had to give it some time.

This poem does not come out of any situation in which I acted the way the lifeguard does in the poem. I did once help dive for a drowned man in a lake where there was public swimming, and I remember going down ten or twelve feet where everything is blacked out. We didn't have any lights and all we could do was to *grope* around for the body. My fingertips *did* turn into stone, and it *was* awfully cold. There was very little chance that I or anyone else could find the body under those conditions. It's a situation I never want to be in again. I was the father of two young boys in those years and was acutely conscious of the protection motif in the human situation.

These things came together in my mind, and I conceived of the situation in which a lifeguard in a summer camp failed to save a little boy from drowning. Little boys have a great belief in the god-like nature of older boys, and they idolize the fellow at summer camp who teaches them to shoot a bow and arrow or takes them on hikes. If one of the little boys goes under during swimming period, all the remaining little boys know that the lifeguard is not going to let anything happen to him. The lifeguard knows where the boy is; the lifeguard has supernatural powers. The poem is told from his point of view. He tries his goddamnedest to get the boy, but he doesn't know where the boy is. When he dives down to where the boy has gone under, he can't see; he can't hear; he can only grope for the boy and hope he finds him before it's too late. But there's little chance that he will, and of course he doesn't. In the terrible chagrin of these circumstances, he hides out in the boathouse. He can't face the children of the boys' camp—or the "village of children," as the poem says—and hides from them

as one child would hide from another child. The only difference is that he is an adolescent of sixteen or seventeen and
they're children. In his delirium of grief as he hides, he comes to
believe that when the children have gone to bed and the moon
shines on the water with enough strength, he'll be able to walk
out onto the water, much as Christ did, and raise the child
back into life. He wishes to undo what has already been done.
That's what we all want to be able to do, isn't it? At the end
of the poem he realizes that he hasn't walked on the water, or
even if in his fantasy he has walked on water, the child he
raises up is not the living child but slips through his hands like
water. Allen Tate once said that he thought of his poems as com-
mentaries on those human situations from which there was no
escape. "The Lifeguard" is my idea of a poem about one of those
human situations from which there is no escape. The little boy
really has drowned. The hallucination and the Christ-image
can sustain the grief-stricken lifeguard for a little while, but at
the end of the poem they break down. The child is now a child
of the water, of water.

THE LIFEGUARD

In a stable of boats I lie still,
From all sleeping children hidden.
The leap of a fish from its shadow
Makes the whole lake instantly tremble.
With my foot on the water, I feel
The moon outside

Take on the utmost of its power.
I rise and go out through the boats.
I set my broad sole upon silver,
On the skin of the sky, on the moonlight,
Stepping outward from earth onto water
In quest of the miracle

This village of children believed
That I could perform as I dived
For one who had sunk from my sight.
I saw his cropped haircut go under.
I leapt, and my steep body flashed
Once, in the sun.

Dark drew all the light from my eyes.
Like a man who explores his death
By the pull of his slow-moving shoulders,
I hung head down in the cold,
Wide-eyed, contained, and alone
Among the weeds,

And my fingertips turned into stone
From clutching immovable blackness.
Time after time I leapt upward
Exploding in breath, and fell back
From the change in the children's faces
At my defeat.

Beneath them I swam to the boathouse
With only my life in my arms
To wait for the lake to shine back
At the risen moon with such power
That my steps on the light of the ripples
Might be sustained.

Beneath me is nothing but brightness
Like the ghost of a snowfield in summer.
As I move toward the center of the lake,
Which is also the center of the moon,
I am thinking of how I may be
The savior of one

Who has already died in my care.
The dark trees fade from around me.
The moon's dust hovers together.

I call softly out, and the child's
Voice answers through blinding water.
Patiently, slowly,

He rises, dilating to break
The surface of stone with his forehead.
He is one I do not remember
Having ever seen in his life.
The ground I stand on is trembling
Upon his smile.

I wash the black mud from my hands.
On a light given off by the grave
I kneel in the quick of the moon
At the heart of a distant forest
And hold in my arms a child
Of water, water, water.

In the poem, "Listening to Foxhounds," the kind of fox-hunting I'm talking about does not involve people chasing foxes around on horseback. I'm talking about the kind that's done in Appalachia. You set your dogs loose on the trail of the fox, then build a fire in the woods and sit around drinking whiskey and listening to the dogs run the fox. All the work is done by the dogs. The men don't do anything but sit there and say: "That's old Belle in the lead," or "That's old Red now." The poem presents a situation in which someone who doesn't have a dog in the race is sitting with the other fellows who do, and he sympathizes with the fox. Well, if you sympathize with the fox in this elite corps of fox-hunting men who all have dogs and are fascinated by the sounds of the dogs, you just don't say anything. Maybe this confers kind of a special privilege on you, and maybe the fox understands why you don't say anything. But when the fox escapes, as the poem says, "it is hard/ . . . To keep that singing down." The poem is predicated pretty much ea; maybe it's a little obvious or too pat, but it seemed good idea at the time.

Heaven of Animals" has been written about a good deal, I'm told. There's a long essay on it, for example, in a book by Paul Carroll called *The Poem in Its Skin*. He has a most ingenious explanation of the poem. It surely was very revealing to me, I can tell you.

I have always been interested not so much in utopias, but in heavens, eternal places. As I've said before, I think the ordinary conception of heaven might make it a very boring place. I would like to know what eternity is like! I don't really believe there is any, or any conscious one at least. But the fact that men have held the idea of heaven, or some kind of eternal life, for such a long time in so many different ways gives the concept a certain authenticity, I think. I have always tried very hard to understand what kind of heaven I would be interested in living in, myself. I wrote an essay on Marianne Moore from the standpoint of her possible construction of a heaven. I would like to have Marianne Moore construct a heaven! I would trust her more than anybody else. I would rather live in her heaven than T. S. Eliot's, for example.

As nearly as I can remember, the idea of "The Heaven of Animals" came to me when I was watching a Disney film. I love those Disney nature films, like *Nature's Half Acre*, *The Living Desert*, *White Wilderness*, and *The African Lion*. *White Wilderness* has that marvelous twenty-minute sequence on the year of the wolverine which I like better than anything I've ever seen on film. I could see it twenty-four hours a day every day. And *The African Lion* has that terrific sequence on the cheetah getting up full-speed to chase down an antelope. They have a telephoto lens on the cheetah that can hardly follow him, he's going so fast. These enormous leaps! Just marvelous! In fact, I saw *The African Lion* so many times that my children wouldn't even go with me anymore. There is one scene in it where a leopard is up in a tree and a herd of wildebeest comes by. He drags down one of the young and eats it. But you know good old Disney; this has got to be made okay for the kiddies. So while the wildebeest is being rended limb from limb, the unctuous voice of the announcer is saying that it's all part of the great cycle of nature. Nothing is wasted; even the young of the vultures are fed. And the camera pans up to show the vultures eating the meat. Now it's pretty hard to explain to the animal being chewed up that this is all part of the cycle of nature! He wouldn't be very interested in such philosophical pronouncements, I'm sure. Nevertheless, Disney's right anyway, if you want to look at it from his point of view.

I also remember reading, at about the same time, Thomas Aquinas, who has a long explanation in one of his innumerable works about why animals have no souls: why only men have souls. This idea has always seemed manifestly unjust to me. I think any living thing ought to be credited with a soul. If one species is, then they all ought to be. So these three things, my speculation about heaven, the Disney sequence in *The African Lion* of the leopard killing the wildebeest calf, and Aquinas's theory about souls, began to work together in my mind; and I thought, "Poets can upset philosophers' ideas, at least in their poems, so why don't I write about what happens to an animal when it dies?" In the poem I say:

> Having no souls, they have come
> Anyway, beyond their knowing.

Then I asked myself what kind of heaven an animal would live in. I decided it would have to be something like his environment except for a couple of important changes. I wanted each beast to have his own identity: that is, the lion would not really be a lion if, as the Bible says, the lion lies down with the lamb. It would be the form of the lion but not the spirit. I wondered what kind of heaven there could be in which the hunted would still be hunted and the hunters would still hunt. I pondered this a long time, and thought there really was no solution because it would be too self-contradictory. "No wonder God gave up on it!" I thought. But eventually I came up with what I felt was quite a good solution: the hunter would still hunt and strike down his prey, but the hunted animal wouldn't be killed and would get up again. So I wrote the poem around that idea. I made it very simple.

From the Disney announcer I got the idea of the cycle of nature. It seemed to me that maybe heaven would be at the center of the cycle rather than on the periphery, or as Eliot says, it would be "At the still point," which would be timeless.

I wrote this poem in an advertising office. I had a new secretary and I asked her to type it for me. She typed up the poem letter-perfect and brought it to me. Then she asked, "What is it? What company does it go to?"

"This is a poem," I said.

"It is?"

"Yes, it is, I hope."

"What are we going to sell with it?" she asked.

"God," I said. "We're going to sell God."

"Does this go to a religious magazine or something?"

"No, I'm going to publish it in *The New Yorker*," I told her. And, as it happened, that's where it came out.

THE HEAVEN OF ANIMALS

Here they are. The soft eyes open.
If they have lived in a wood
It is a wood.
If they have lived on plains
It is grass rolling
Under their feet forever.

Having no souls, they have come,
Anyway, beyond their knowing.
Their instincts wholly bloom
And they rise.
The soft eyes open.

To match them, the landscape flowers,
Outdoing, desperately
Outdoing what is required:
The richest wood,
The deepest field.

For some of these,
It could not be the place
It is, without blood.
These hunt, as they have done,
But with claws and teeth grown perfect,

More deadly than they can believe.
They stalk more silently,
And crouch on the limbs of trees,
And their descent
Upon the bright backs of their prey

May take years
In a sovereign floating of joy.
And those that are hunted
Know this as their life,
Their reward: to walk

Under such trees in full knowledge
Of what is in glory above them,
And to feel no fear,
But acceptance, compliance.
Fulfilling themselves without pain

At the cycle's center,
They tremble, they walk
Under the tree,
They fall, they are torn,
They rise, they walk again.

"A Birth" is a short poem about continuity and also about the capacity of the imagination to alter the real world. A man who wants to write a poem about a horse imagines a horse in a field. This is the way many poems start, I suppose. But then at a certain point the horse is no longer subject to the poet's mental restrictions and just walks away and becomes real. The poet finds himself in a room with his mother and his child, in the middle of the three generations. He sits there, not saying anything, and feels the nature of reality changing, because the horse that he imagined has now been added to the totality of living existence.

In *Drowning With Others* I had some poems about hunting, such as "Fog Envelops the Animals" and "For the Nightly Ascent of the Hunter Orion Over a Forest Clearing." I hadn't done very much hunting at the time, but I began to be interested in it because I had always liked the woods. But I had never liked guns. It has always seemed to me that an important relationship between men and animals has to be a life-or-death relationship. It's no good to take a camera into the woods and photograph animals. I think an animal is debased by that. I think you've got to go in there and try to kill him. The odds are against you, especially if you're using a weapon like the bow and arrow. My luck has been notoriously bad! What matters to me is to *be* there, not to be there just walking in the woods, but to be there in that specific kind of life-or-death relationship. One could say, "Yes, *their* death! But *you're* not risking anything!" But you *are*. A man raised in the suburbs—I'm anything but an expert woodsman—is taking a definite chance, going into the woods. I have very little sense of direction; I get lost easily. It rains. You can fall and break your leg. Dreadful things can happen when you're five or six miles back from the road in some remote area. So you're not safe at all, yourself.

And the wilder the territory is, the larger the animals are. I ran into a large bear last fall, for example. Scared me to death!

But the main thing is to re-enter the cycle of the man who hunts for his food. Now this may be play-acting at being a primitive man, but it's better than not having any rapport with the animal at all. We come from an ancient lineage of people who hunted their food and depended on the meat, skins, sinews, and gut of animals. In my case at least, I have a great sense of renewal when I am able to go into the woods and hunt with a bow and arrow, to enter into the animals' world in this way. The animals don't change. It wouldn't make any difference to them whether I was an Indian hunting them or a suburbanite with sharpened steel broad-head arrows. In the final analysis I can't explain why I respond so much to hunting with a bow and arrow or why Hemingway responded so much to big game hunting or watching bullfighting. After all, you may hear a song, like the tune, and it may come to mean a great deal to you but not mean much to anybody else. It's very largely a question of what you respond to.

At any rate, "Fog Envelops the Animals" is about hunting. In the poem, fog rolls up and envelops the protagonist, who is in a white outfit, maybe long underwear or a white camouflage suit. He feels himself become invisible. We all want to be invisible, at least part of the time, but most especially the hunter does. Concealment for the archery hunter is the greatest thing of all. In this case, the hunter, being exactly the same color as the fog, has total concealment. As long as he can see enough to shoot, but the animals can't see him, he's in heaven.

"In the Tree House at Night" is another family poem, another way of getting at the kind of continuity that exists in families by the passing of some kind of skill or enterprise from one member of the family to another. It has obvious affinities with "The String," for example, where the family passes the string tricks from one generation to another. In this case, an older brother built a tree house and told the two smaller boys that when they got bigger all of them were going to build a big tree house in the highest tree of all, up there where he pointed his hammer. But the older brother has died and now the middle brother, who feels himself the recipient of the older brother's legacy of building the tree house, feels constrained to build it for all of them. The poem is an account of his building it, nailing the slats on the pine tree and going up little by little. Building a tree house is terrific fun, and very dangerous also. He takes his little brother up as a kind of fulfillment of what the dead older brother wished them all to do. As the two brothers are lying in their blankets and the wind is blowing the tree back and forth, the middle brother feels the presence of the older brother there. It's one of those recognition scenes where you don't know whether it's a real recognition or just something you dreamed up yourself. He doesn't know whether his dead brother is actually present or not, but he feels that if he isn't present then, he's not likely to be present under any other conditions: he *has* to be there, with them, in their *place*.

"The Owl King" is a fantasy that was suggested by a phrase in a book by the French poet, Loys Masson. The phrase was *Le roi des hiboux,* the king of the owls. And I thought, "I don't want to read any more of this guy's poetry; that's enough." I wanted to be able to take off from that phrase, and for better or worse that's what I did. I first wrote a poem called "The Call" in which a father has lost his blind child in the woods. The way you would call a blind son back from the woods probably would not be quite the way you would call a son who could see. It might be some kind of song that the father himself would become enamored of, not knowing he could make such a sound. "The Call," which became the first part of a three-part poem, "The Owl King," was originally published by *The Hudson Review.*

By the time it came out, I was already working on the second and third sections. So I thought, "All right, you have a situation here with the father trying to furnish his blind son with an audible point of reference toward which the child can come, some kind of continuous sound. Then the owl himself would be in the woods, and what would he be like? There is also the boy." So it fell into a three-part poem. The second part is called "The Owl King," and the third part "The Blind Child's Story." The title, "The Blind Child's Story," is a conscious parody on the kind of thing that Hollywood does all the time, *The Rocky Graziano Story* or *The Ernie Pyle Story*; I took the convention and used it.

Then I began to imagine the Owl King himself. (I like owls.) I thought, "This is the Owl King, no ordinary owl; he's the quintessential owl, the immortal owl; the only thing he fears is the sun. Maybe I can make him kind of a Nietzschean owl who is able to see in the dark by an act of will over a long period of time." As I said earlier, when you have an idea that interests you, you should commit yourself to it completely, and not have any reservations about it. This is very important in my own practice, and I would hope it would be in anybody else's practice too. So I committed myself to a Nietzschean owl who has taught himself to see by a long and extremely intense act of the will, so that he wakes up one evening in the woods and can see in the dark. I asked myself what it would be like, and I imagined that the owl would be looking out and could see a little farther each time. And what would he see? He would see all the predatory animals and the snake, like the Euroboros, the form of all life; and he would see the fox, and the animal that is preyed upon. I thought it would be good to show what the owl wanted to do with his existence, and what he did, from his own point of view. He eventually controls the night forest completely because he's the only one who can see and fly.

Then the child comes into the forest, for no specified reason except that children are always running off from the house, and he encounters the Owl King. The owl takes him up into the tree and teaches him to see. Whether or not the child really sees as a result of his encounter with the Owl King, or whether the owl is only a fantasy on the part of the child or the father or both of them, I would just as soon leave up to the reader. But if you take the poem literally, the owl *does* teach the child to see, and the boy comes back and sees his father for the first time, standing there howling in the moonlight like an animal in love with the sound of his voice. The end of the poem is supposed to be an act of total acceptance of the world through the figure of the child.

Again, if you want to think of this as silly, nothing could be sillier. You might ask, "Why should a grown man waste his time writing this kind of thing? It doesn't happen; it doesn't have anything to do with 'the world we live in.'" But that doesn't seem to me to be relevant at all. If you want to write about the Owl King and the blind child, even if they put you in the nut house, you should be privileged to do it!

"Between Two Prisoners" is the only other poem I ever wrote about Don Armstrong and Jim Lalley, who were taken prisoner by the Japanese and beheaded. We learned a lot of gruesome details about their deaths from the Filipino guerrillas. They were kept in an old schoolhouse and tied up with wire. I don't know exactly how you would tie somebody up with wire, maybe just wrap it around him. It seems terribly cruel to bind someone with wire. But the main thing is that they were put into a schoolhouse and evidently sat in desks. The Japanese bound them to the abandoned desks of Filipino school children. I tried to imagine them in the desks, wounded, surrounded by the blackboard and all the school paraphernalia. This would affect them very much, and they would talk. There would be an enormous importance to words, because they couldn't act. And this might also in some mysterious way affect the guard who was watching over them until their execution the next morning. He would be affected although he didn't understand a word. He would know that something essentially human was passing back and forth between these two bound, doomed men in the classroom. I used the device of the blackboard to try to figure forth what the guard might have seen as a result of these two fellows being in the classroom under these dreadful conditions.

The poem ends, of course, with the execution of the guard. War crimes are very strange things. Who knows who's guilty of what? Who knows where responsibility ends, and duty and patriotism begin? The Nuremberg trials, I understand, hold a man responsible for his actions, and if he doesn't want to burn up Jews in the furnaces he must tell his superiors he won't do it. But actually, for the Japanese guard, that attitude would serve no purpose. If he didn't go along with it, somebody else who would be quite happy to go along with it would immediately replace him.

I didn't want to show the guard as an inhumane person, but one who was simply caught in this situation. And although he might have been profoundly affected by the prisonership of these two fliers in the schoolhouse, and even changed, even made a saint by it, it didn't matter to the war crimes people. He was one of those responsible for the execution. This is against the Geneva Convention, and therefore he was hanged. I was very interested in trying to imagine what he might have seen under the hangman's hood as he dropped through the trap door. Would he have seen the blackboard again and the figure of the angel? Again, maybe I'm trying to talk the poem into existence. But as I said earlier, I'm only talking from the standpoint of what I attempted to do in the poem, what I hoped others would see.

There is another poem in *Drowning With Others* that I like. It's about the ancient whorehouse in Pompeii. I was in Pompeii with my wife and child, and this wily Italian guide said, "Let your wife and child go along. I want to show you something, just between us men." He took me into the Lupanar and said, "This is the Pompeiian *whora housa*." It was the best preserved building in Pompeii, oddly enough. He showed me how the women would go up on the roof and signal to passers-by. There was a fine engraved penis in the flagstone pointing the way. He showed me how they sold tickets. Then he said, "Now, over each of these seven cubicles there is a fresco of each of the seven different positions." He shined his flashlight around the walls, and behold, there they were! I said, "Might I be left alone for a moment?"

He told me that some of the couples had died *in medias res*. What a way to go! In the poem I sit there and try to imagine what it would be like to be in the Lupanario and die from the eruption of Vesuvius. It's a common misconception that the people in Pompeii were buried under lava; actually they died from inhaling the ashes and suffocating. I tried to get that bit of archaeological information into the poem. "In the Lupanar at Pompeii" became a poem about the hopeful attitude we all have toward passion, not only sexual passion, but passionate experience. We don't want to live and die as zombies. We want to be capable of some true passion, sexual or any other kind, at least once, instead of just experiencing the standardized brand. We want to be able to give ourselves completely, whether it's to a prostitute or anybody or anything else. We want a total act of the body, true passion rather than just a routine milking of the glands.

"Drowning With Others" was a poem I wrote because I liked the title. I wanted to call the book *Drowning With Others*, so I decided I'd better write a poem by the same title to give some status to the book's title. I don't think it's a very strong poem; it seems awfully obscure to me. But the general idea is that when there are a group of people in the middle of the

ocean after a shipwreck with no life boats or life jackets, one
by one they're going to drown. They're going to give up trying
to stay alive; one by one they're going to go down under your
feet, and you will see them spiraling down under the sea. It
seems to me that the essential human act is for you to try to
keep somebody else up, even though you're all going to die.
And the person that you try to keep up for a few minutes
longer is the person that tried to keep you up, even though
there's no hope for anybody. You are drowning with others.
That constitutes to me a symbol of the essential humanity of
all of us at our best: that we can try to help someone even
though nothing can save either of us.

"The Hospital Window" is another family poem, a father-
and-son poem in which the father is dying of cancer. I think
of that as the most dreadful thing to die of: a slow, wasting
death. In the poem the son has gone up to the hospital room to
confer for a while with his father. But as the poem begins the
son has come away from his father realizing that he can't say
what sons ought to be able to say at these times. He has been
in the hospital—one of those dreadful antiseptic places where
we go because there's no other place to go, and where occasionally a few people are saved—trying to say to his father that unsayable thing that one hopes to be able to say, but which nobody since the beginning of time has ever been able to say.
So he goes down from the sixth floor in the elevator and out
into the street, unsatisfied. He turns around to look at the hospital and thinks that if he can find his father's room and get
some kind of signal from him, just a wave of the hand, then
maybe the unsayable would have been said. So he stands in
the middle of the street and holds up traffic. He could care
less about traffic! The traffic backs up on both sides of him,
horns blowing, and he just stands and waves at the hospital.
Everybody in the hospital seems to be looking out, because a

lot of people wave at him "from inside their flames." The sunlight is shining from the glass front of the hospital. Finally his father gives him a weak gesture and he goes, satisfied with that, because he has to be.

He thinks about his father's blue eyes and the fact that his father could look out, not afraid, at his crazed son in the middle of the street and wave at him as though this were perfectly natural. If you're not afraid for the life of your son who's standing in the middle of a lot of high-powered automobiles, then surely you're not afraid of your own death from cancer. Whether or not this is true, the son takes it as a sign and goes away. He takes renewed strength from the fact that he's his father's son and that he may himself have the qualities he imputes to his father, whether or not they really are there in either. I think illusion is a very great part of human existence; it enables you to bear up under the circumstances that you have to face.

"The Salt Marsh" is about the terrors and ways of being reconciled with nature. There are salt marshes on the southern coastal plains, for instance on the coast of Georgia south of Savannah or Brunswick. If you go into a marsh, there's no possible way to know what your direction is, especially at noon. Once you go into the weeds, which are higher than your head, there's no way of knowing where you are. I think the feeling of being lost is the most frightening feeling there is; you literally don't know what to do. You can see yourself in one of those frightening flash-forwards you have in these situations, stumbling around in the mud for days with nobody knowing where you are. I was actually lost like this once. The sawgrass is so resilient, it will cut the devil out of you. You can hack it down—I didn't have a machete or knife with me—but you can't beat it down; it just springs right back up. When it closes around you, you can't see anything but grass blades. You don't know where the ocean is; you don't know where the land you came from is. That's a terrifying, terrifying feeling. But it's only terrifying if your attitude is that the grass is against you. When the wind begins to blow, though, all the grass leans to one side in an enormous whispering movement. Then it's possible for a certain kind of person to have an entirely different feeling about the alien quality of the grass.

I tried to contrast these two feelings. At first when you are in the salt marsh you can only look straight up. You can see the birds fly overhead; but it gives you an even greater feeling of imprisonment to compare the birds' freedom with your own mud-sucking attempts to walk through the marsh, surrounded by grass and terrified of snakes. But then the wind blows and the sense of *participation* in the grass is just unearthly. I think it's one of the most beautiful feelings I've ever had. For me, the next thing to a river in beauty is to see some kind of grain blow in the wind. Keats, I was delighted to find out, also loved this. When he was a child, he used to watch the wheat fields, or whatever they grew in the part of England where he went to school, and would cry out when the wind began to blow, "The tide! The tide!" And it seems to me that a person lost in the marsh would have a kind of conversion to nature when he realized that nobody was there watching him and he was absolutely anonymous in the reeds. So when the wind blew and the sawgrass bent, he could bend also. It probably would even help him get out of the marsh, too, because his morale would be changed and he would then be able to view his situation with more resourcefulness. I wasn't, of course, trying to write a poem about how to get out of the sawgrass, but about two different kinds of experience, two different attitudes toward the same situation.

The last poem in *Drowning With Others* is "In the Mountain Tent." It's about an unorthodox view of religious things, and is something like "The Salt Marsh" in being about solitude. I believe that amazing things can happen if you get far enough away from other people. I believe that you *do* odd things you would ordinarily never do if you had a companion or knew somebody was watching you. You have a different personality.

"In the Mountain Tent" is about a man way off in the woods, in what the maps call a "roadless area," who is sleeping in a tent in the rain. He knows that the only creatures around him are animals. As he's lying there, he begins to dream of his own death. I don't know whether he's a Christian or not, but being a product of Western culture, he's influenced by Christian doctrines and the belief in Resurrection. And so he feels both a great kinship with the animals on the mountainside with him in the rain and a fundamental difference from them, because he realizes that he may rise from the dead and they'll only die.

There's a great deal of difference between this poem and "The Heaven of Animals," but it's not up to the poet at all to be consistent. It is his privilege to look at a subject from two opposite standpoints. You shouldn't expect a consistent philosophical attitude from a poet. Some such may emerge from his work. But I think it's a serious mistake on the poet's part to try to make his work coherent as far as a rational structure is concerned. Because really a poet like myself is writing about experiences and ideas based on them. Any kind of self-consistency would be fine if it simply happens, but I don't think the poet should seek it out. I would agree with Emerson that a foolish consistency is the hobgoblin of little minds. Look at someone like Yvor Winters, the primary example of the poet who writes by the rules. When he writes a poem, he knows pretty much what he's going to do, which things he's going to deem admissable, and which not. The result is a very narrow, restricted kind of verse, exercise stuff. The ideas may be perfectly consistent, but the poetry is no good. The larger consistency that the body of a poet's work should have, should come from the totality of the poet's personality, including all its contradictions. It took me a long time to find that out.

Chapter III

Helmets

Once a curious thing happened to me. I was reading in Indiana. *Helmets*, my third book, had just come out. A little red-headed girl came up to me and wanted me to autograph *Helmets*. I opened the book to try to find a place to autograph it, but the whole book was covered with annotations—every page. There were more annotations than poems, and I couldn't find a place to sign my name. I turned back in desperation to the dedication page. It was dedicated "To Maxine: *light and warmth.*" And behold, the dedication was annotated! She had a little line going from "light" that said "intellectual," and one from "warmth" that said "physical." I suppose that's what I meant, but it seemed strange with all that scholarly apparatus.

Helmets was an attempt to deepen some of the themes that I had announced in *Into the Stone,* but mainly in *Drowning With Others.* The hunting theme took on a much greater importance, and I wanted to get back to the war theme in a way which had nothing to do with flying. I don't think I wrote anything in *Helmets* about flying. I wrote about the war from the standpoint of the infantry where you have a much closer intimacy with what happens to the *people* in a war. For example, "Drinking From a Helmet" deals with being in the center of action, between the enemy and the graveyard. The incident occurred on Okinawa where we were fighting on Coral Ridge and the graves registration people were about two hundred yards in the rear laying out a cemetery that the fellows fighting up on the ridge would soon be occupying. This was one of the weirdest sights I ever saw. I wanted to write at least one poem about that kind of physical involvement instead of using the terrific and terrifying detachment of the combat aviator—I later wrote about that subject in a poem called "The Firebombing."

So the book, *Helmets,* was an attempt at intensifying some of the things I had already announced. I thought that the best way for me to move was not toward a number of other lyric poems about the subjects I wanted to deal with, but rather toward an attempt, in William James's great phrase, to turn "the cube of reality," to show the same action from different sides as seen or imagined by one person.

"Chenille" is a poem about north Georgia. Dalton, Georgia, is known as "the Chenille Capital of the world." I used to ride through there whenever I got a chance, because I like Dalton and the mountain country up around there. But it has a sad history of industrialization. I don't think there's anything sadder than country boys working in factories. It doesn't seem right for *those* kinds of people to be working in cotton and textile mills.

You can go by the Dalton mills, and all along the highway there are chenille bedspreads for sale, hanging on clotheslines. Apparently the pattern never changes. There are almost always two peacocks on the bedspread. Sometimes there's a mallard or a flamingo. I don't know why folks in the country are so attracted to flamingos. You see those little artificial flamingos in people's yards. Flamingos are very weird creatures, but the peacock is an officially pretty bird. I suppose that's why the peacock ends up on so many chenille bedspreads, because everybody knows it's pretty. The industrial process produces a very stylized, conventional-looking kind of peacock.

In this poem I wanted to write about official beauty versus unofficial beauty. I've known those old chenille mills and bedspreads all my life. But one winter I was hunting way up north of Atlanta, and I got lost, as usual. It was getting dark and cold and beginning to rain, so I went to a farmer's house and asked if I could stay there and pay for a bed. He told me to come in. His grandmother was living with his family, and she was making a design on a chenille spread. I kept looking at it. It was a crazy-looking thing, like an elephant with great pink wings. I asked her what it was. "Just something I made up," she said. "I thought it would be pretty."

Then I asked her, "Ma'am, do you think things like this really exist in the world?"

"Of course they do," she said, "because they ought to." She showed me some more spreads. There were what looked like mythological creatures, strange-looking things like the griffin and the basilisk and the phoenix. There were also some deer, but most were curious concoctions of her own. Finally, picking up the elephant bedspread, I went up to bed in the top of the house.

I started getting cold in the middle of the night—Lord, it was cold!—but I didn't know how to get any more covers. Then I dozed off again and wasn't cold anymore. When I woke up in the morning, I was covered with chenille bedspreads. The old lady or somebody had thrown them on top of me. I was just covered with them! I looked at them one after another. It was like looking at a picture book, the elephants and the ants with crowns and all the mythological creatures. In writing the poem, I contrasted the industrial chenille spreads with the spreads produced by the half-demented imagination of this old lady. Maybe it's too obvious a contrast, but it seemed to me wonderfully symbolic of the artistic process, of art produced by the creative mind versus the officialized kind of beauty. And I wrote the poem pretty quickly on that basis.

"Springer Mountain" is another poem about being alone in the woods. It's about the wild, hopeful conjunction between the wild animal and the archery hunter who experiences an extraordinary kind of transport. I don't think there's anything more exciting in the world than first spotting an animal like a deer in the woods. I remember Dick Steiglitz, a fellow I used to hunt with in Atlanta, saying to me before I went bow-hunting with him, "Boy, wait till you see the first deer in the woods! You'll have to hold onto a tree to keep from taking off!" It must be something like what happens to skin divers. Divers become enormously exhilarated—I suppose from breathing that nitrogenized air—and feel wonderfully brotherly toward the fish. They may take their masks off and offer them to the fish as evidence of their marvelous rapport with them. What sometimes happens in the woods is like that. You see the deer moving off between the trees, and . . . well. Everything is changed.

But *I* never took off my clothes and entered into a ritual dance with the animal I'd been trying to kill. *I* never did anything like this, but I aspire to it. After all, the ultimate homage to the hunted animal is to enter into his world, to kneel down naked like a beast and drink from a spring in weather so cold you feel like you're frozen in a block of air. You don't even have the fur of an animal; your genitals ache, and the marrow of your bones seems to harden. Just to be in the animal's world you suffer much more than he does. Then you go and hunt him, probably without success. But you pay him that homage too, of entering with him into the kingdom of life and death, into the eternal cycle of predatory animals and those hunted by the predators. Again, this might seem unimportant in the world of the atomic bomb, but to me it is important.

SPRINGER MOUNTAIN

Four sweaters are woven upon me,
All black, all sweating and waiting,
And a sheepherder's coat's wool hood,

Buttoned strainingly, holds my eyes
With their sight deepfrozen outside them
From their gaze toward a single tree.
I am here where I never have been,
In the limbs of my warmest clothes,
Waiting for light to crawl, weakly
From leaf to dead leaf onto leaf
Down the western side of the mountain.
Deer sleeping in light far above me

Have already woken, and moved,
In step with the sun moving strangely
Down toward the dark knit of my thicket
Where my breath takes shape on the air
Like a white helmet come from the lungs.
The one tree I hope for goes inward
And reaches the limbs of its gold.
My eyesight hangs partly between
Two twigs on the upslanting ground,
Then steps like a god from the dead
Wet of a half-rotted oak log
Steeply into the full of my brow.
My thighbones groaningly break

Upward, releasing my body
To climb, and to find among humus
New insteps made of snapped sticks.
On my back the faggot of arrows
Rattles and scratches its feathers.

I go up over logs slowly
On my painfully reborn legs,
My ears putting out vast hearing
Among the invisible animals,

Passing under thin branches held still,
Kept formed all night as they were
By the thought of predictable light.
The sun comes openly in
To my mouth, and is blown out white,

But no deer is anywhere near me.
I sit down and wait as in darkness.

The sweat goes dead at the roots

Of my hair: a deer is created
Descending, then standing and looking.
The sun stands and waits for his horns

To move. I may be there, also,
Between them, in head bones uplifted
Like a man in an animal tree
Nailed until light comes:
A dream of the unfeared hunter
Who has formed in his brain in the dark
And rose with light into his horns,
Naked, and I have turned younger

At forty than I ever have been.
I hang my longbow on a branch.
The buck leaps away and then stops,
And I step forward, stepping out

Of my shadow and pulling over
My head one dark heavy sweater
After another, my dungarees falling
Till they can be kicked away,
Boots, socks, all that is on me
Off. The world catches fire.
I put an unbearable light
Into breath skinned alive of its garments:
I think, beginning with laurel,

Like a beast loving
With the whole god bone of his horns:
The green of excess is upon me
Like deer in fir thickets in winter
Stamping and dreaming of men
Who will kneel with them naked to break

The ice from streams with their faces
And drink from the lifespring of beasts.
He is moving. I am with him

Down the shuddering hillside moving
Through trees and around, inside
And out of stumps and groves
Of laurel and slash pine,
Through hip-searing branches and thorn
Brakes, unprotected and sure,
Winding down to the waters of life
Where they stand petrified in a creek bed
Yet melt and flow from the hills
At the touch of an animal visage,

Rejoicing wherever I come to
With the gold of my breast unwrapped,
My crazed laughter pure as good church-cloth,
My brain dazed and pointed with trying
To grow horns, glad that it cannot,
For a few steps deep in the dance
Of what I most am and should be
And can be only once in this life.
He is gone below, and I limp
To look for my clothes in the world,

A middle-aged, softening man
Grinning and shaking his head
In amazement to last him forever.
I put on the warm-bodied wool,
The four sweaters inside out,
The bootlaces dangling and tripping,

Then pick my tense bow off the limb
And turn with the unwinding hooftracks,
In my good, tricked clothes,
To hunt, under Springer Mountain,
Deer for the first and last time.

"Cherrylog Road" is a much-anthologized piece. I think it's sort of funny and innocent. It seems to me to have a Huckleberry Finn quality about it, even though it deals with motorcycles and junk yards. What I attempted to show by means of a boy and girl having a sexual rendezvous in an old junk yard full of bootleggers' cars and wrecked stock cars was that magical moment when you realize that this year you can do a lot of things you couldn't do last year. You know, last year you were riding around on a bicycle, and this year you've got a big, powerful motorcycle.

Junk yards are oddly surrealistic. Growth is heavy in the South. If junked automobiles are left in a lot, it's going to look like a jungle in a few months, especially in summertime. Kudzu vines will be growing through the cars; and snakes, turtles, roaches, mice, toads—everything you can think of—will be living there. It is a strange place for human love; where man's castoff goods and nature meet. And I suppose the factual experience is changed somewhat simply by virtue of writing about it in one way rather than another. I don't think Cherrylog Road was the name of the road. It's a place name I picked up on a fishing trip I took one time, but it seemed like a good name. I realize it doesn't matter whether the incidents in a poem are true, but people might be interested to know that in this case they really are.

"The Scarred Girl" is another personal interpretation of an incident that happened when I was in high school. I knew a girl who was the prettiest girl in Atlanta, by far. She was not pretty in a sexy way, but she had a Madonna-like beauty, that kind of soft, shining, lustrous-eyed quality—I never saw such eyes in a human head! I used to dance with her occasionally around Atlanta, but I never knew her very well. The most wonderful thing I remember about her was that she was very good. Most pretty girls are bitches, but she was a lovely, sincere, helpful person. It was not an affectation; she really *was* good. She went with a boy who was not in her class at all, I thought. Then of all things, he got into an automobile wreck, and she went through the windshield headfirst. It cut her face into absolute hamburger; she had to have years of plastic surgery. She never looked anything like she had before.

This seemed terribly tragic to me. I've been brooding about it for thirty years. I had been reading in Plato about the Good, the True, and the Beautiful. This girl was true—although she seemed almost too good to be true—and good and beautiful she surely had been. It struck me that when a woman who is only beautiful loses her beauty through an accident or through age, she has had literally everything taken away from her. But she had this marvelous resource of being good, too. So the beauty had been taken away by the wreck, but she still had this goodness, as I say at the end of the poem, that is now "the only way." It *was* the only way and, I suppose, still is. The events of the poem really do seem to lead to a conclusion of this sort. I don't generalize in poems very much; I would rather present. But I did make an exception in this one.

"The Poisoned Man" is a snake poem. The poem is allegorical; I didn't see any way to avoid that. It's about a farmer who is bitten by a rattlesnake and cuts open the sole of his foot and puts it in a cold mountain stream. I read in a book that when you cut open a snake bite, it's necessary to keep the blood flowing. The blood wavering from his foot into the current takes the path of the serpent, as the poem says. The poem becomes an allegory—maybe too obvious an allegory— about the fall of Man, because the blood poisons the stream, and the trees and crops die, and he and his wife have to leave his farm like Adam and Eve leaving the Garden of Eden. Again, this may be too much of a one-to-one correspondence. As James Merrill wrote to me when the poem came out in

The New Yorker, "I thought it was very good, but I do seem to have heard that story somewhere before." And he had, he had!

Whitman cautioned American poets to have nothing more to do with myths that had been used a million times before, when he said that they should give over those enormously overpaid accounts of the War of Troy, Achilles' wrath, and so on. But I think the one lesson you can learn from poetry, if you take it seriously enough, have enough luck, and work hard at it, is that the ancient Biblical and Greek myths are always reclaimable if you can bring something new to them. Look at Yeats's "Leda and the Swan." That poem is marvelous in its immediacy, its feeling of power and spontaneity, and especially in the interpretation that Yeats puts upon it because he's Yeats. The ancient myths are always accessible if you have the poetic power to bring that kind of renewal to them. I don't make any great claims for "The Poisoned Man," but it certainly was part of my intention to treat myth in this way.

"In the Marble Quarry" comes from my advertising days when I was working for Liller, Neal, Battle and Lindsey. I was doing a story or an ad for a holding company called the Southern Company. A very good photographer, Jay Leviton, and I went up to Tate, Georgia, where there are enormous marble quarries. One quarry was about half a mile across, and I could see that, before somebody had started quarrying, it was just woods and fields like the rest of the landscape. The trees came right up to the edge where men had sliced through to make the quarry. Some of the roots were literally sticking out over the abyss of marble. That's why I call it "the undermined wood" in the poem. I arranged to go down into the quarry and was lowered down about five hundred feet on a cable. The fellows on the bottom were cutting out big blocks of marble with power saws. I started talking to the foreman and asked him what the marble was used for. He said it was used for government buildings and banks, but most of it was used for tombstones. I thought, "Lord, isn't that strange? I'm down here in the land of the tombstones, where they're born."

After I had all the information I wanted, the foreman told me that they were sending up a twelve-ton block and I could ride up on it. So I got up on the block, and they started hoisting it. On the way up I looked around me, as I hadn't done on the way down, and I could see time stratified at the different geological levels. So I thought about that as I rode up on the block of marble that was going to be somebody's tombstone, maybe mine. And although I'm not sure, I might also have thought at that time of Michelangelo's great statement about sculpture. Somebody asked him how he created all those beautiful statues out of stone. He replied that the questioner had a misconception about what happens in sculpture, or at least in *his* sculpture. The form was already in the marble, and all he did was chip away the stone from around it. And I thought maybe that was true of my tombstone. I wondered what the figure in the marble was like if it was my tombstone. In the poem I have the speaker imagine that the figure in stone is:

> Badly cut, local-looking and totally uninspired,
> Not a masterwork
>
> Or even worth seeing at all
> But the spirit of this place just the same,
> Felt here as joy.

"The Being" is a poem unlike most of mine. Figure a man who is sleeping on a winter night and is being possessed by something. He doesn't know whether it's a human woman who gets into bed with him or a succubus—a mythological creature who co-habits with sleeping men and takes their energy—or whether it's an angel or some kind of renewing spirit of the year. I deliberately did not explain what it was, because when you have these visitations, as sometimes happens, the whole point is that you don't know whether it's a dream or what. It's all of these things and none of them. But the experience in the poem is definitely meant to be sexual and has not so much the effect of robbing the sleeper of his powers as of being a kind of purgation of the winter's ills and a presage of the spring's renewal. M. L. Rosenthal has written very perceptively about this poem. It may be that he sees some things in it that I don't, but I would refer you to his book, *The New Poets: American and British Poetry Since World War II*. I think he's the only critic who mentions "The Being."

I suppose "Approaching Prayer" is the most complicated and far-fetched poem I've written. Surely it's very far-fetched. But when you're trying to write about miracles—and prayer is a miracle if it's anything—it's not like having a conversation with a stenographer; miracles *are* far-fetched. They are the most out-of-the-ordinary things that could possibly be. In this poem I tried to imagine how a rather prosaic person would prepare himself for the miraculous event which will be the prayer he's going to try to pray. His father has died, and he thinks his father is going to have something to do with the prayer. So he gets a couple of his father's artifacts and also something of his own, a boar's head. The most out-of-the-ordinary thing he ever did was to kill a huge wild boar with a bow and arrow, hunting him with dogs and shooting him in a creek bed. He goes up to the attic, puts on the hollow boar's head and his father's sweater. With him he also has gamecock spurs that once belonged to his father. Then he kneels under the skylight in the attic of the empty house and believes he has shed his reason and is far enough from ordinary life to be able to pray, *really*. He feels something go through him. He doesn't know whether this is his prayer reaching its object, God, or some kind of supernatural being, or whether it is something physical happening to him like a nerve pulsation. But he feels satisfied that he has either prayed or come as close to prayer as he can. Then he puts down the boar's head, goes away, and never comes back. He has approached prayer. Whether he has attained it or not is another thing.

In World War II I was in some awfully harrowing action in the Pacific, and in some places I didn't think it would be possible to survive at all. The result is that now, far removed from those scenes, places, and events, I view existence pretty much from the standpoint of a survivor—sort of like a perpetual convalescent. Someone wrote an article on me once which was called, "James Dickey, the Grateful Survivor," and I can very well affirm that this is my attitude. It's really the only personal philosophical implication of the war that I can think of, although there doubtless are a good many others I'm not aware of consciously.

I think physical courage is a very, very great thing, though. I've always thought so. Injuries are terrible. Anybody who will stand up to possible injury, either to help someone else or to perform some kind of mission is a great man to me. I feel very much as Malraux does or Antoine de St. Expuréry did. I'm not a worshiper of duty in the way that St. Expuréry was at all, but I very much admire dependability, which involves some degree of courage.

I've already said something about "Drinking From a Helmet," a poem about being in war and close to destruction. The poem deals with a boy's first inkling that his attitude is going to be that of a grateful survivor if he survives this day. He's drinking water and identifying with the soldiers lying in the graveyard who have not been as lucky as he. He dedicates himself to survival and to looking up the brother of the dead soldier whose last thought he inherited by drinking from the dead man's helmet and putting it on afterwards.

Chapter IV

Buckdancer's Choice

"The Firebombing" has been commented-on a great deal. What other people have said about it is more ingenious and more thorough, I believe, than anything I can say, except that the poem concerns a very complex state of mind, guilt at the inability to feel guilt. In poems, and elsewhere, it's very easy to abase yourself and be terribly guilty over your own or somebody else's warlike actions. Take that sententious poem by Stephen Spender called "On the Pilots Who Destroyed Germany in the Spring of 1945." At the end of the poem the spectator, a civilian who is in no danger because he's not going on the mission says that, though his life "never paid the price of their wounds," it yet "assumes their guilt, honors, repents, prays for them." Spender doesn't do anything of the sort! He may pray for them, but he doesn't assume their guilt. That's an easy and cheap poeticism. It's fashionable to talk about guilt in poems, like Sylvia Plath feeling guilty over the slaughter of the Jews. She didn't have anything to do with it. She can be *sorry*, but guilt is more personal than that: it has to do with something you have *done*, or could have done and didn't. It's a literary convention for her. To have guilt you've got to earn guilt, but sometimes when you earn it, you don't feel the guilt you ought to have. And that's what "The Firebombing" is about.

There's a God-like feeling about fighting on our planet. It's useless to deny it; there is, or at least some of the time there is. You can never do anything in your life that will give you such a feeling of consequence and of performing a dangerous and essential part in a great cause as fighting in a world war. The greatness is not only in an ideological sense, but exists also simply because millions of people are involved in the event. To say that it's wrong to feel this way is not the point; you *do* feel it. This poem deals with a kind of guilt which results from the inability to feel anything but elation upon remembering destructive acts. There were a lot of people in the service, for example, who cried when they were discharged because they knew they would have to go back to driving taxis and working in insurance offices. For them there wouldn't be any more of that *kind* of excitement, and above all, there wouldn't be any more consequence. They wouldn't be heroes or even potential heroes then; they would only be ordinary human beings. You feel a nostalgia for war because all the intensities of life, youth, danger and the heroic dimension, as nearly as you will ever know them in your own personal existence, were in those days.

The protagonist of "The Firebombing" is a suburban householder bowed down with making payments, keeping track of his children's toys, getting his sons to scout meetings, mowing the lawn, and all those inconsequential things we all do: these things are our lives. He can hardly believe he is the same person who got into that night aircraft and took off with napalm bombs on bomb shackles under the wings. This memory produces an extremely complex state of mind. He's now a householder, and he realizes with a shock that he's burned up women and children with napalm in his God-like phase. He's wondering how it felt for those people, but he can't really imagine it. They were Japanese, about as foreign to him and his origins as anything could possibly be. But most importantly he can't imagine the result of the mission because he never saw it.

In aerial warfare you can't contemplate the results of your

destruction, especially at night, because they are hidden from you by distance and darkness. All you see is a flash of fire and, depending on your altitude, you don't even see that sometimes. You have a terrifying detachment from the result of what you are doing. If you had gone down there and seen your destruction of these people, then you would be able to feel guilt, easily. But it's in the nature of the operational function you're performing that you can't do this, even if you wanted to. This detachment produces a peculiar state of mind. The protagonist feels that his inability to imagine one of his victims knocking at his door with his ears burned off, his inability to imagine anybody knocking at his door except his neighbor coming over to borrow the lawn mower, is a kind of judgment on him—and it is. He is realistic about it, though, and says that there is nothing he can do; and there isn't. Maybe that's the worst sentence of all, to be deprived of feeling what a human being ought to be entitled to feel.

"Buckdancer's Choice" derives partly from my mother's invalidism and partly from a guitar showpiece I try to play, a fast picking piece called "Buckdancer's Choice." I remember my mother lying in bed whistling to herself when she got tired of listening to the radio; she had to rest eighteen hours a day. I don't know where she picked it up, but she had a beautiful warble. I loved to hear her. In some strange way I connected her whistling with the old minstrel shows where the tune "Buckdancer's Choice" originally came from. A buckdancer is a buck-and-wing dancer, the principal dancer of the old-time minstrel shows. Buck-and-wing developed in the days of slavery. After the Civil War minstrel shows were very popular, and ex-slaves who had danced on the plantations participated in a lot of them.

I tried to get all those elements together; the invalid mother with a heart condition, and the dying tradition of minstrel shows revived in this woman's incidental whistling of the old-time minstrel show music, "Buckdancer's Choice," which the little boy overhears at her door without her knowing.

"Reincarnation (I)" and "Reincarnation (II)" were written at widely divergent points in time. They were both part of an idea I hope to go back to eventually, a series of poems called "Reincarnations." Reincarnation is one religious idea I have always loved believing in. I don't know whether the soul passes from one kind of creature to another; I hope it does. I would live this human life gladly if I knew I was going to be a bird—next time—or have any kind of consciousness at all. That would be terrific! I think there's a great deal to be said for the idea of transubstantiation of souls in Hindu religions like Jainism. I was going to write a poem about reincarnations up through the evolutionary ladder from the very lowest forms: man being reincarnated as a mollusc, then up through the fish and amphibian kingdoms to the mammals, and finally man being reincarnated as a man: as himself, maybe, even. But I didn't get very far; I only wrote about a snake and an albatross. If I were to undertake the series again, I don't think I would include either one of these poems. They seem too independent to fit very easily into any kind of sequence.

I thought "Reincarnation (I)," the poem about a man being reincarnated as a rattlesnake, was a good idea. I had been getting tired of the three-beat line, for I had already written the better part of three books in it. I thought I might try a longer line just to see what would happen. So I put an arbitrary limit on the line of "Reincarnation (I)." I simply wrote as far across the page as the typewriter would go, and that was essentially the line. It didn't take me as long as usual to write this poem; it just seemed to make itself up.

I wrote the poem at the time when there began to be a lot of agitation in Mississippi. I don't know whether it was before or after the murder of those three civil rights workers involving Sheriff Rainey and Deputy Cecil Price. It might have been a little before this, but the idea of the injustice of a great deal of Southern justice might have been in my mind to some extent. I thought it might be a good idea to leave a hint that the man who had been reincarnated as a rattlesnake was one of those kinds of people, because the symbol of the snake has to do with justice. It's not only the symbol of the medical profession, the snake twined around the staff. The justice of the Lord, in its most striking case, depended on the intervention of the snake. I wanted, if possible, for all of that to be implicit. I didn't want to thrust it at the reader, but that's one reason I made the snake a judge.

The main thing that interested me in writing this poem was the transformation that would occur in the process of reincarnation. You would give up your human form, your head, arms, and teeth, and take on the long snake body. I wondered how it would feel when the human consciousness would be slowly dying out and the snake would be gradually coming to, lying in an old cartwheel by the side of a river. The remnants of his human identity would be leaving him, and he'd now begin to understand what it would mean to be a snake: that is, to be poisonous. He'd still have something against men and would wait for somebody to come by so he could bite him.

"Them, Crying" is about hospitals. I've always had the most complete horror of hospitals. I can't walk into the door of a hospital without beginning to shake uncontrollably. I view hospitals as charnel houses. I don't know why this is, because they're places of mercy and we'd obviously be in bad shape without them. But it seems we're in bad shape with them, too. I hold it against doctors that they're not miracle workers; they're helpless in so many ways. They're trying, and eventually they'll be doing better, but they're mainly helpless. For a doctor to tell me that the person I love has something that nothing can be done about makes me feel murderous. Why *can't* he do anything; isn't he a doctor? That's obviously a childish attitude, but it's very much the way I feel about the whole medical profession. This poem also is about unreason. Some kinds of unreason are a lot better than reason, I think.

My own son, Chris, had his arm broken in one of those unfair collisions between an automobile and a bicycle when we were living in Oregon, and he was in the children's ward in some hospital. We got just a glimpse of him every now and then. The doctors kept us out of there; I suppose we might have upset him or the hospital routine. But we would sit on a bench for hours at a time, and the nurses would go in and out of the children's ward, but the parents were never allowed to go in. I was completely cowed, like the rest of the parents who had children in the ward. But I would sit there at one or two at night and could hear the children crying in there with nobody to comfort them. And I thought, "I'm going to get up my courage one of these days and go in there and see if I can do something for those children. They're terrified, waking from operations and accidents when the sedation wears off. It's terrible to leave those children like that." I never did get the courage. But one night a drunk guy staggered in—looked like a truck driver—and went right into the children's ward. It said *No Admittance,* but he went right in. And I thought, "You're my man! That's a heroic thing to do!" To this day I don't know who he was. I hadn't seen him before. I assume that if he had a child who was related to him in there, he would have been around before. But he just came in the middle of the night, went in and stayed a while, and then came back out. That was all I ever saw of him.

To me, the voice of a child who is alone, frightened, and in pain is an appeal so powerful that it can go through any barrier and be heard anywhere. So to make this kind of situation as extreme as it is and the appeal of the children's voices as powerful as it is, I made a truck driver driving a rig on the highway hear them. There was no choice; he had to go where they were:

> . . . for these [the children] rise only unto
> Those few who transcend themselves,
> The superhuman tenderness of strangers.

"The Celebration" is another poem that is pretty much autobiographical. In high school I went to a carnival at Lakewood Park near Atlanta. I was just walking along in the crowd among the gambling wheels, strip teasers, and carney games, when I looked up and saw a man and a woman. She had on an old fur coat, and he had a walking stick and a Stetson hat. I thought, "If I didn't know it was so impossible, that would look very much like my mother and father." I looked at the couple again, and that's who it was! I couldn't have been more surprised if it had been Jesus Christ and John the Baptist. They were walking there like fifty-year-old lovers. My father was swaggering a bit and my mother was holding onto his arm. It was the sweetest thing, I swear to God, I ever saw in my life! I wondered what in the world was going on. They had never been particularly demonstrative or affectionate with each other. I decided to follow them around to see what they would do. They went on the Tunnel of Love, and he won a teddy bear for her throwing baseballs at milk bottles. Then they went on the Ferris wheel. I just stood there watching my mother and father go around and around in the air. They never did know I was within miles of the place.

There's an absolute strangeness of a situation in which you see people you thought you knew so well acting like complete strangers—and you thought you could never find out anything new about them! I guess there's nobody more familiar to most people than their mother and father. But the experience I had made me feel an enormous kinship to them, based partly on the fact that they hadn't revealed everything to me and I had by accident discovered not only something about them but something about myself that I hadn't sufficiently reckoned with.

By the way, the local reference about the condemned train climbing up a track is an actual reference to the Lakewood Amusement Park. They used to have a roller-coaster there called "The Greyhound." It's been condemned since 1910, so naturally everybody wants to ride it. And everything at the carnival is in some way circular. The gambling wheels, or the carney Come On In are all circular, and all the rides end where they begin; and of course, the Wheel of wheels is the Ferris wheel. You can see it from all over the fair, the lights going around like Ezekiel's wheel in the middle of the air. All carnivals and midways are circular and wheel-like, in one way or another.

"The Escape" is a wish-fulfillment poem. I'm so claustrophobic that I have a horror of burial, especially in a cemetery —at least in an ordinary cemetery. Again, I never bought a grave plot in the country for myself. But since I wrote the poem, I now have given myself the idea of doing so. And I probably will do it. The cemetery in the city is a sad, sad environment where the hospital, textile mills, and the city have grown up around what used to be a village graveyard. The hospital attendants come into the cemetery to eat their lunch, and girls from the textile mills walk by.

The speaker in the poem is buoyed-up by the fact that he has escaped from that cemetery. He has resolved not to be buried in that place where his family is buried. He remembers an incident when he was hunting and came upon a little country graveyard. In the country there's a custom of having a big simulated Bible at funerals. It's a pasteboard imitation of a Bible that is empty except for two real pages with passages of scripture written in hand, like "I am the Resurrection and the Life. . . ."

Part of the poem deals with an incident that really happened to me. I *did* see a Bible like this in a country graveyard, and I wanted to go over to read the words, but something stopped me from going into the cemetery. I looked up and saw a little spike buck walking through. He went over and looked at the book lying on the new grave. The book had evidently been put there that morning because there was no dew on it. Of course, when the first rain comes the book will crumble up and be washed away. That's why the poem refers to "the fragile book/ Of the new dead" "before the first blotting rain." So this would be the speaker's only chance to read the words on the Bible. But he doesn't, because he wants to imagine that they are from Genesis.

"The Shark's Parlor" is completely made up. I never heard of anything like it happening nor did I participate in anything like it. When I was a boy I *did* see some boys fishing with a sashcord in the south coastal part of Georgia. I suppose people use poles now, but when I was a kid down there on the ocean, all I ever used was a hand line. I still like to fish with a hand line, because your fingers are more sensitive to the feel of the fish taking the hook than if you use a rod. In the poem the boys are using a giganticized form of the hand line; instead of a cord they use a rope, and instead of a bobber they use a sealed glass jug. If you're fishing for shark, as the boys are, you use a thin steel chain as a leader so he can't bite it in two and a big cruel shark hook with a piece of rancid meat on it. The more blood and meat you can scatter around, the better chance you have of catching a shark. You get a bucket of blood and guts at the slaughter house, bait your hook, and row out in a boat as far as your cord will reach. You row out to the channel where most of the big fish are, put the hook and jug in the water, and spill the guts and blood around the hook to attract sharks. Then you go back to the shore to wait for the jug to be pulled under the water. In the poem I mention Cumberland Island, but what little I remember of these practices was on St. Simon's Island, Georgia, near Brunswick. The boys in the poem bait their hook with a "run-over collie pup," which I thought was a very gruesome detail.

"The Shark's Parlor," like "Cherrylog Road," is about a *rite de passage,* that is, growing up through some kind of traumatic experience. These fellows are trying to be big boys, drinking beer for the first time and sitting on the porch of a house watching for an enormous shark to take their hook. The necessity for kids, especially boys, to overmatch themselves, to take on more than they are qualified to handle, seems to me absolutely characteristic of male youth. The poem shows this, I think. And it describes how they mishandle everything. Everybody gets hysterical. They end up dragging the shark into the house; he wrecks it and is finally thrown out. But the poem is not so much about the actual incident as it happened *then,* but as the man who took part in it remembers it—what it meant to him then and what it means to him now. The terrific energy of the primitive creature and its blood have sanctified the house for him, and he has bought the house and lives in it. As an older man he realizes that this is the reason he bought the house: for the symbolic charge of energy it has come to have for him. It still has some of the shark's blood on the wall, and not many houses have shark's blood on the wall! Now that the man is growing older, he realizes in retrospect what significance this event has, for it has become full of implications that he would never have thought of as a boy.

One interesting point about houses like the one described in the poem is that they are built on stilts, because the ocean's tide comes in fast and often rises five or six feet under the houses. And I am sure that sleeping in a house with the ocean underneath is different from sleeping in a house above land. I tried to get some of that feeling into the poem, as well as the other ideas about adolescence and the taking-on of powers you're not certain yet how to use, and are also uncertain that you have.

I made "Fathers and Sons" into a two-part sequence: one in which the father is killed and the son survives, and the other in which the son is killed and the father survives. I've always loved the first poem, "The Second Sleep," but I don't think anybody else has ever paid much attention to it. Most people seem fonder of the second one about the father's loss, "The Aura." My own boy, Chris, was almost killed in his bicycle accident. I really was terrified he was going to die from shock or loss of blood. I would sit in the hospital—the same hospital that was more or less the background for "Them, Crying"—and try desperately to characterize Chris to myself. What was it about him that I remembered the most? It finally turned out to be that he always had music around him, usually on his body, with a transistor radio. He loved the Beatles, the Rolling Stones, and that kind of music so much that he could never bear to be without them. Everywhere he went the Beatles went. It was this constant aura of music he carried on his body that was, to me, the most indicative thing about him, the most *him*.

So I made that the subject of "The Aura," except that in the poem the boy dies and the father tries to possess the memory of the boy. What he remembers is the kind of music the boy carried around on his person: the sound that used to wake the father up in the morning as it went wandering into other rooms of the house. Sometimes the music was very loud and sometimes he could barely hear it, but always it was there. So after the boy's death he begins to seek out the music that characterizes his son, and he discovers that he can find it anywhere, in department stores and in bars where his son would have gone, in a couple of years, to drink beer. Maybe this is not much consolation, but he comes to believe that it's surely better than nothing. It's painful, but it's still better than the void that was there and would otherwise be there, without the music.

"Sled Burial, Dream Ceremony" has been variously interpreted. I don't really know myself how to interpret it except that it's a poem about death, but the death of a particular kind of person, an American Southerner. Southerners are always mystified by the customs of people who live where there's a lot of snow. Except in travels, I've never seen much snow in my life. Snow is exotic to a Southerner.

It seems to me that death is really the most foreign thing from what your life has been. In this poem I made a little drama in which the Southerner, in order to be fully dead, would have to enter into the country of snow where people who were the most foreign to him lived. The poem describes a ritual in which he arrives on a train in his coffin and is taken on a sled by these people, who are wrapped in scarves to keep their heads warm, to a lake where a door is cut in the ice, and he is buried in the lake. The Southerner then knows he is truly dead, because he is in the ultimate foreignness.

"The Night Pool" is a poem that I have a great deal of affection for, because it says some of the things about love that I want to say. People generally think of love as a violent emotion, a situation where the lovers go from peak to peak of intensity. The most spectacular quality of love is this intensity, sexual as well as other kinds. But for me—I don't know how other people feel about it—the main thing I characterize as the emotion of love is the wish to protect the other person.

Swimming pools are very erotic places to me, especially at night when nothing is real. There's a frail, eerie light that comes up from the underwater lights at the sides of the pool. The situation in the poem is based on this feeling, and on a real incident. In October several years ago a girl and I went swimming in a pool at the apartment complex where she lived in Atlanta. The pool was going to be drained in a few days, and there was nobody in it because it was too cold. But it was a heated pool and the steam was rising from it when we went in at about two o'clock in the morning. Nobody else came. There were only one or two lights on in the apartments; everybody else was asleep. And it was just magical! All your earthly debts are canceled while you are in a heated pool in the middle of a cold night. Nothing that you have to contend with in day-to-day life is there. You don't even have your weight any more. You can perform prodigious feats: the man can lift the girl up in the water as if she were hardly there at all, and the girl can lift the man up. They can do court dances and water ballets around each other, and it's dream-like and lovely. You're in the warm, amniotic fluid of the pool, comfortable and protected, and the effect is superhuman. You never want to leave.

But then, as Jonathan Winters might say, there comes a time when "you gotta get out!" It's cold and the weight of the world hits you like a sledgehammer. You think the world has no right to do this to you after you've been so comfortable and erotic. It's the unsexiest possible situation: the girl is stringy-haired and freezing to death, and so are you. It's miserable. But that is the time when love is really love, when you wrap her up and protect her. You can stand it yourself, but you don't want her to have to stand it. So you "wrap her in many towels," and if you love her, you should.

THE NIGHT POOL

There is this other element that shines
At night near human dwellings, glows like wool
From the sides of itself, far down:

From the deep end of heated water
I am moving toward her, first swimming,
Then touching my light feet to the floor,

Rising like steam from the surface
To take her in my arms, beneath the one window
Still giving off unsleeping light.

There is this other element, it being late
Enough, and in it I lift her, and can carry
Her over any threshold in the world,

Into any of these houses, apartments,
Her shoulders streaming, or above them
Into the mythical palaces. Her body lies

In my arms like a child's, not drowned,
Not drowned, and I float with her off
My feet. We are here; we move differently,

Sustained, closer together, not weighing
On ourselves or on each other, not near fish
Or anything but light, the one human light

From above that we lie in, breathing
Its precious abandoned gold. We rise out
Into our frozen land-bodies, and her lips

Turn blue, sealed against me. What I can do
In the unforgivable cold, in the least
Sustaining of all brute worlds, is to say

Nothing, not ask forgiveness, but only
Give her all that in my condition
I own, wrap her in many towels.

"The War Wound" is a rather unambitious little poem. I have a half-moon-shaped cut on my hand that I got when I was in an airplane wreck. I was given the Purple Heart for it because it was suffered in action. It wasn't a bad cut; it didn't even require stitches. One of the planes I was in made a wheels-up landing. I was sitting in the co-pilot's seat and when I reached up to protect myself, my hand was cut on the instrument panel.

I sometimes would look at my hand and think, "Lord, the war that killed and mutilated so many people did only *this* to me!" But that is my war wound, anyway. I thought that a wound which came out of a world-wide experience like the war ought to have some magical properties. It ought not to be like other wounds because perhaps one hundred million people contributed to it in some way. I asked myself what kind of magical property I would like it to have. And I decided that now as a middle-aged suburban householder I would like it to warn me when my children were in some kind of danger. So I wrote the poem around that sort of far-fetched idea. The wound is small, but it has in it the fury of the world in convulsion. It's my souvenir of "the war of the millions," and must be unlike other scars I have.

I've always liked the writing of John Updike because, for one reason, he takes the high school experience seriously. For example, in *The Centaur* he takes as a hero the high school science teacher, Caldwell, and identifies him with Chiron the Centaur. I can't presume to speak for the girls, but I can surely say that the high school experience is absolutely formative in the case of boys. I think failure in athletics is one of the most terrible things that can happen to a person. I was sort of neutral in high school, poised between success and failure. In the same way the failure of a girl to become beautiful during the high school years, to be neglected by the more hand-some and virile boys, must be terrible.

Anyway, in the poem, "Mangham," I tried to regard the high school experience seriously. I had a teacher at North Fulton High School named Mr. Mangham, a gray, undistinguished man but an extremely good mathematics teacher. What happens, though, when you're an extremely good mathematics teacher and nobody cares about learning mathematics? We had a class in which Mr. Mangham would teach trigonometry assiduously every day, and we would more or less go through the motions of learning it. But this was all changed when he had a stroke one day in the classroom; he died a week later. At the time I never thought anything of this in particular. I never had any feeling for Mr. Mangham. He seemed sort of a gray nonentity to me, like most high school teachers seem to most high school students. But he had held out through the class period. He got some ice cubes from the cafeteria, held them to his face, and hung in there with his Law of Cosines and those things he was dedicated to. Now when I'm at the age Mr. Mangham was when he had the stroke in class, his action seems to me as heroic as Leonidas at Thermopylae, because he was holding onto his "thing." He was dying; he was paralyzed on one side, but be-cause he was a teacher of trigonometry he was going out with his boots on. He was teaching trigonometry to people who had no aptitude or liking for mathematics, who were simply taking it as another required subject. To "do your thing," as the hippies say, in the face of that kind of indifference, seems to me to be absolutely heroic.

I wrote the poem around that idea as a tribute from one of Mr. Mangham's indifferent students whom he wouldn't even rec-ognize if he could come back as an angel on the wings of the Pythagorean theory. But I remember the class and I re-member his rear-guard action against oblivion, arming himself with the Law of Cosines. That seems wonderful to me. It didn't then, but it does now.

"The Fiend" has been a much-attacked poem. It also has been much-anthologized. As I said earlier, I think the idealization of women is indigenous to men. There are various ways of idealizing women, especially sexually, based in almost every case on their inaccessibility. If you go to see a skin show in Las Vegas, the women seem much more important as sexual objects because they're not accessible to you. It's always rather giving the game away when you have a real woman with you in a hotel or motel room, and she takes off her clothes. I don't think there ever lived a man who didn't have a dreadful qualm of misgiving, thinking, "Oh, is this all there is?" It's only a few inches of mucous membrane after all! But when a woman functions as an unobtainable love object, then she takes on a mythological quality. You can see this principle functioning as a sales device in advertising and in places like *Playboy* magazine. Almost every movie you see has this quality, because you can't embrace the image on the screen. Thousands of novels use this principle, because you can't embrace a printed image on a page. But the person who most truly understands this principle, whether he would be able to put it exactly in these terms or not, is the voyeur. There's something of the voyeur in every man. Every man would like to see a good-looking woman undress, especially if she doesn't know he's there. It's important to the voyeur to have an invisibility that enables him to function in kind of a God-like way, as though he could be present at any scene, sexually or otherwise, that he wished to be present at. I wanted to enter the mind of the voyeur, with some of these considerations, just to see what would happen.

The nicest letter I ever received from anybody was in connection with this poem when it appeared in the *Partisan Review*

a few years ago. Someone wrote me a letter from New York
with no return address or signature. It said:

> Dear Mr. Dickey:
>
> I can't give you my name or return address, so you won't be
> able to answer this. But I'd like you to know that I'm a mem-
> ber of the Special Vice Investigation Squad of the New York
> Police Department, and I read your poem, "The Fiend," in the
> *Partisan Review*. I just want you to know that I've always had
> a lot of secret sympathy with you fellows.

The amazing thing to me in retrospect is not so much that
he wrote me about the poem, but rather, what on earth was a
member of the Vice Squad of the New York City Police
Department doing reading the *Partisan Review?* Anyway, I
took the letter as a kind of compliment, because evidently the
policeman was convinced that every word of it was true.

But it wasn't true. I never did anything like that, although,
as I said in connection with an earlier poem, I aspire to it.
The poem deals with a homicidal voyeur. I'm anything but
that, although I may be selling myself short—I don't know!
But sexual idealization is an awfully important idea. The fantasy life is probably the most important thing that men have;
it's much more important to them than reality. Reality is only
an adjunct to the fantasy lives of most men. I won't presume
to speak for women. But voyeurism, *"Playboy*-ism," pornog-
raphy, and things of this sort contribute, as David Riesman in-
dicates—I mentioned this before—to the enrichment of fantasy.
You really *live* in your fantasy life. That's where your deepest
concerns and your main intensity lie.

So the voyeur in my poem, "The Fiend," with his knife in
his pocket and his other characteristics is really an idealist
in the purest sense. He will go to any lengths to see a girl
naked, whether she is a shopgirl or a society woman. He'll wait

patiently, like an animal, until the magical moment comes when she starts to take a shower. He'll climb up to the top of a tall tree beside an apartment house to see her. That's a lovely dedication, I think. In the poem I also wanted to show that women, with their great hunger to be idealized, might feel something of this extreme, concentrated idealism coming in from the night where the voyeur in the tree would be having his transports of ecstasy. The woman would feel that she was on a kind of stage, and it would be a wonderful sexual experience for her. Because she's not being just looked at; she's being *beheld*, which is different. The poem reaches a climax when the voyeur actually goes in and murders her because of the continual frustration of not being able to behold her.

Of course, the poem can be taken as the maunderings of a poet who is a sex monster himself but who has never killed anybody, or at least has never been apprehended for it. It could easily be and has been taken for this. But I would have no interest whatever in writing poems if I couldn't follow my impulses to some kind of *reductio ad absurdum*. If I want to write a poem about a sexual monster, or a voyeur, up in a tree, then that's just going to have to be the way it is. As long as the law doesn't forbid me to do it, that's what I'm going to do.

THE FIEND

He has only to pass by a tree   moodily walking   head down
A worried accountant   not with it   and he is swarming
He is gliding up the underside light of leaves   upfloating
In a seersucker suit   passing window after window of her building.
He finds her at last, chewing gum   talking on the telephone.
The wind sways him softly   comfortably sighing   she must bathe
Or sleep.   She gets up, and he follows her along the branch
Into another room.   She stands there for a moment   and the teddy bear
On the bed feels its guts spin as she takes it by the leg and tosses

It off.   She touches one button at her throat, and rigor mortis
Slithers into his pockets, making everything there—keys, pen
and secret love—stand up.   He brings from those depths the knife
And flicks it open   it glints on the moon one time   carries
Through the dead walls   making a wormy static on the TV screen.
He parts the swarm of gnats that live excitedly at this perilous level
Parts the rarefied light high windows give out into inhabited trees
Opens his lower body to the moon.   This night the apartments are
    sinking

To ground level   burying their sleepers in the soil   burying all
    floors
But the one where a sullen shopgirl gets ready to take a shower,
Her hair in rigid curlers, and the rest.   When she gives up
Her aqua terry-cloth robe the wind quits in mid-tree   the birds
Freeze to their perches round his head   a purely human light
Comes out of a one-man oak   around her an energy field   she stands
Rooted   not turning to anything else   then begins to move like a
    saint
Her stressed nipples rising like things about to crawl off her   as he
    gets
A hold on himself.   With that clasp she changes   senses
    something

Some breath through the fragile walls   some all-seeing eye
Of God   some touch that enfolds her body   some hand come up
    out of roots
That carries her as she moves   swaying   at this rare height.
    She wraps
The curtain around her and streams.   The room fades.   Then
    coming
Forth magnificently   the window blurred from within   she moves
    in a cloud
Chamber   the tree in the oak currents sailing   in clear air keeping
    pace
With her white breathless closet—he sees her mistily part her lips
As if singing to him, come up from river-fog   almost hears her as if
She sang alone in a cloud   its warmed light streaming into his branches

Out through the gauze glass of the window.   She takes off her
    bathing cap
The tree with him ascending   himself and the birds all moving
In darkness together   crumbling the bark in their claws.
By this time he holds in his awkward, subtle limbs the limbs

Of a hundred understanding trees.   He has learned what a plant is
    like
When it moves near a human habitation   moving closer the later it is
Unfurling its leaves near bedrooms   still keeping its wilderness life
Twigs covering his body with only one way out   for his eyes into
    inner light
Of a chosen window   living with them night after night   watching
Watching with them at times their favorite TV shows   learning—
Though now and then he hears a faint sound: gunshot, bombing,
Building-fall—how to read lips: the lips of laconic cowboys
Bank robbers   old and young doctors tense-faced   gesturing savagely
In wards and corridors   like reading the lips of the dead

The lips of men interrupting the program at the wrong time
To sell you a good used car on the Night Owl Show   men silently
    reporting
The news out the window.   But the living as well, three-dimensioned,
Silent as the small gray dead, must sleep at last   must save their lives
By taking off their clothes. It is his beholding that saves them:
God help the dweller in windowless basements   the one obsessed
With drawing curtains this night. At three o'clock in the morning
He descends   a medium-sized shadow   while that one sleeps and
    turns
In her high bed in loss   as he goes limb by limb   quietly down
The trunk with one lighted side. Ground upon which he could not
    explain
His presence he walks with toes uncurled from branches, his
    bird-movements
Dying hard. At the sidewalk he changes   gains weight   a solid
    citizen

Once more. At apartments there is less danger from dogs, but he has
For those a super-quiet hand   a hand to calm sparrows and rivers,
And watchdogs in half-tended bushes lie with him watching their
    women
Undress   the dog's honest eyes and the man's the same pure beast's
Comprehending the same essentials. Not one of these beheld would
    ever give
Him a second look   but he gives them all a first look that goes
On and on   conferring immortality while it lasts   while the
    suburb's leaves
Hold still enough   while whatever dog he has with him holds its
    breath
Yet seems to thick-pant   impatient as he with the indifferent men
Drifting in and out of the rooms   or staying on, too tired to move
Reading the sports page   dozing   plainly unworthy   for what
    women want
Dwells in bushes and trees: what they want is to look outward,

To look with the light streaming into the April limbs   to stand
    straighter
While their husbands' lips dry out   feeling that something is there
That could dwell in no earthly house: that in poplar trees or beneath
The warped roundabout of the clothesline   in the sordid disorder
Of communal backyards   some being is there in the shrubs
Sitting comfortably on a child's striped rubber ball filled with rainwater
Muffling his glasses with a small studious hand against a sudden
Flash of houselight from within   or flash from himself   a needle's
    eye
Uncontrollable   blaze of uncompromised being. Ah, the lingerie
Hung in the bathroom! The domestic motions of single girls living
    together
A plump girl girding her loins against her moon-summoned blood:
In that moon he stands   the only male lit by it, covered with
    leaf-shapes.
He coughs, and the smallest root responds   and in his lust he is set
By the wind in motion. That movement can restore the green eyes
Of middle age   looking   renewed   through the qualified light

Not quite reaching him where he stands again on the usual branch
Of his oldest love   his tie not loosened   a plastic shield
In his breast pocket full of pencils and ballpoint pens given him by
      salesmen
His hat correctly placed to shade his eyes   a natural gambler's tilt
And in summer wears an eyeshade   a straw hat Caribbean style.
In some guise or other he is near them when they are weeping without
      sound
When the teen-age son has quit school   when the girl has broken up
With the basketball star   when the banker walks out on his wife.
He sees mothers counsel desperately with pulsing girls face down
On beds full of overstuffed beasts   see men dress as women
In ante-bellum costumes with bonnets   sees doctors come, looking
      oddly
Like himself   though inside the houses   worming a medical arm
Up under the cringing covers   sees children put angrily to bed
Sees one told an invisible fairy story   with lips moving silently as his
Are also moving   the book's few pages bright. It will take years
But at last he will shed his leaves   burn his roots   give up
Invisibility   will step out   will make himself known to the one
He cannot see loosen her blouse   take off luxuriously   with lips
Compressed against her mouth-stain   her dress   her stockings
Her magic underwear.   To that one he will come   up frustrated
      pines
Down alleys   through window blinds   blind windows   kitchen
      doors
On summer evenings. It will be something small that sets him off:
Perhaps a pair of lace pants on a clothesline   gradually losing
Water to the sun   filling out in the warm light with a well-rounded
Feminine wind as he watches   having spent so many sleepless nights
Because of her   because of her hand on a shade always coming down
In his face   not leaving even a shadow stripped naked upon the
      brown paper
Waiting for her now in a green outdated car with a final declaration
Of love   pretending to read   and when she comes and takes down
Her pants, he will casually follow her in   like a door-to-door salesman

The godlike movement of trees stiffening with him   the light
Of a hundred favored windows   gone wrong somewhere in his glasses
Where his knocked-off panama hat was   in his painfully vanishing
    hair.

"Slave Quarters" has to do with Southerners. It concerns
a man who is living in the land which once held slaves, except that nobody within a couple of generations of him has
ever held slaves. He is living in the residue of the slave-owning
culture with all its attendant glory, terror, and ultimate irres-
olution. He's on a Georgia coastal island where he visits the
ruins of a plantation. There really is a place on the coast
of Georgia like this where there are remnants of slave quarters
and you can see the approximate spot where the big house
stood; there's nothing left of that. Maybe there's some kind
of poetic justice in the fact that the owner's house no longer
exists but there are a few remnants of shell-walled slave
quarters.

In this poem I meant to strike right to the heart of the
hypocrisy of slavery and show some of the pity and terror of
it. In the first part of the nineteenth century the South was
committed to a false kind of chivalry and a false kind of Sir
Walter Scott ethic. In other words, while the slave owner in
the great house was giving his daughter piano lessons and
telling her that sweat is unlady-like, he himself was going
out into the slave quarters and cohabiting with one of the
women he had purchased. Now this is a terrible kind of
dichotomy and a hypocrisy very near to being ultimate. My
point is that this kind of schizophrenic attitude, of doing one
thing in public and another in private, is impossible to live
with. I also meant to say in the poem that in this terrible
gentility of the Southern plantation ethos the slave owner
might have gotten—and I'm quite sure in a number of real

instances *did* get—a terrific renewal of his primitive vital functions from cohabiting with slave women. It was not just "fucking," although that might have been true in some cases. But I'm quite sure that in many cases there was a great resurgence of the thing that had damned near been emasculated by all the stultifying gentility the Old South had committed itself to: the pseudo-English, phony gentility that Southerners with their dreadful kind of inferiority complex insisted on emulating. They were not aristocracy, but they tried to pretend that they were, and they tried to pretend that the bodily functions didn't exist. They thought it was degrading to have any kind of pleasure in sexual intercourse. Of course, it's always the women who are the most avid to go along with that sort of thing. The South was essentially a matriarchy anyway. But the Southern planter, becoming his uninhibited male self at night in slave quarters with some woman whom he had purchased and whom he used, would in some sense renew his masculinity and vitality. This is one paradox.

There's another paradox: that he could "raise up seed," as the Bible says, to this woman and have a child by her. If you were an owner of a big plantation and had only daughters, this in itself would be kind of humiliating, despite the fact that the culture was matriarchal. But suppose your only son was by a slave woman and had been conceived in this extremely clandestine manner? What would you do when you looked at that boy? He would be your only son, and he would be out there with all the other slaves cutting sawgrass. You couldn't acknowledge him; you couldn't take him up in your arms and say, "My son, my son, would God I had died for thee!" You would simply own him like all your other slaves. What kind of guilt would that be? This situation seemed to me to be a commentary on the white man's dilemma, but also on the dilemma of the Negro who came out of such circumstances.

It's a problem that is going to take an awfully long time to resolve. It's at the same time so profoundly natural, based on human sexual instincts, and so terribly unnatural, that there is no easy solution. None.

Chapter V

Falling

"Reincarnation (II)," the first poem in *Falling*, is about an office worker who is reincarnated as a migratory sea bird. I'm interested in instinctual processes and the way, for example, that certain kinds of albatrosses can navigate for thousands of miles by celestial navigation. I think that, to human beings, it's absolutely unknowable how they do this, but the point is that they do it. In this poem I wanted to show the voyage of a man who discovers himself reborn as a sea bird. I thought that maybe in the reincarnation process he could be a bird for a while without realizing what has happened to him. He could go all the way up from the Galápagos Islands into the northern polar regions without having much of a sense of what was happening. The poem begins when he is in the area of the icebergs and comes to realize that this is not a dream he's having, that he really *is* a bird circling around in a completely void area where there are no ships or birds. He realizes that this is not an hallucination; he really *does* have wings and a long beak.

I tried to show two things in the poem: first, the recognition of this being that he's now a bird and no longer a man, and his realization that he can navigate by means of the stars; second, the gradual fading of his identity as a human being through this long voyage. On the long nuptial voyage down from the polar regions toward the Galapagos Islands, where he will mate with another bird to produce bird offspring, he loses the last memories of his human life. When he mates and perpetuates his kind, he becomes completely what he is in this phase of his existence. In one phase he was a man; in this phase he is a bird.

He also has a notion of another instinctual thing, death. Most of the poem has to do with instinctual navigation, and at the end of the poem I try to introduce the supposition that death, for a bird that navigates by instinct, also navigates by instinct and will coincide with him at some distinct point of latitude and longitude. And when they meet, he will be changed into something else. Yes.

"The Sheep Child" comes out of the most horrible thing anybody ever told me in my childhood. A boy named Dick Harris once gave me to understand that a man and a sheep can conceive progeny. I asked him if that was really true and he said, "Oh sure; everybody knows that! Way down on the south side of Atlanta there's this museum, and way back in the corner where nobody would ever look, there's this little thing like a woolly baby in a bottle of alcohol, because those things can't live. I could probably find out where it is, and take you down there and show it to you." He never did, thank God! To this day I'm afraid to run into him again, because he might still take me down there and show it to me! But one day I thought this was a possibility for a poem, and so I wrote it. I took the situation seriously and tried to discover some of the implications of what such beings might be like.

I believe that farm boys develop a kind of private mythology that has the effect of preventing too much of this sort of thing from going on. It doesn't prevent *all* of it, you understand, but it keeps it within reasonable bounds—whatever *they* might be! The first part of the poem is a recounting of the farm boys' legend of the sheep child in the museum. But the second part of the poem is supposed to be spoken by the sheep child himself from his bottle of formaldehyde in the

museum. I don't know what other defects or virtues th
might have, but I think it can hardly be faulted fro
standpoint of originality of viewpoint, at least in the la
section!

I intended no blasphemy or obscenity by this poem at all.
I tried to the best of my ability to write a poem about the
universal need for contact between living creatures that runs
through all of sentient nature and recognizes no boundaries of
species or anything else. Really the heroine of the poem is the
female sheep who accepts the monstrous conjunction and
bears the monstrous child, because in some animal way she
recognizes the need that it is born from. I tried to give the
sheep child himself a double vision of the destiny of man
and animal:

> I saw for a blazing moment
> The great grassy world from both sides,
> Man and beast in the round of their need,
> And the hill wind stirred in my wool,
> My hoof and my hand clasped each other,
> I ate my one meal
> Of milk, and died
> Staring.

What I intended was that this *contra naturum* creature born
from this monstrous, clandestine marriage between a human
being and an animal is not *contra naturum* but very much
naturum. It is evidence of the blind and renewing need for
contact between any kind of living creature with another kind.
This need is much larger than and transcends any kind of
man-made, artificial boundaries. And yet, because of men's
minds and attitudes, men develop a mythology to keep it from
happening. Paradoxically, it's probably just as well that they
do. But when things of this sort happen, it seemed to me to

larger need that I was attempting to com-

o terribly sunburned lovers. I thought
y good representation of the pain that
love relationship—or maybe always at-
I wrote a poem about two lovers who are so
badly sunburned that they can't bear to touch each other, but
who are so much in love that they can't bear not to. I like
to think of this poem as having some affinity with Dante.
The writing may not be in any sense Dantean, but at least the
terrible dilemma the lovers are in might have a connection
with some of the things Dante speaks about in the *Inferno*. I
would be the last person to insist on that parallel; it's just something I like to think about privately.

As I get older I write more and more about sex. Adultery
seems to me to be the most potentially beautiful and fruitful
relationship between men and women, and also the most
calamitous and destructive. It's no good saying that adultery
is bad, because some of it is so obviously good. There's no
reason that a married person, or a person who gets beyond
a certain age, shouldn't want love for love without the en-
cumbrances of taking care of children and making payments
on the car. Not love with responsibility, but love without
responsibility; just sex and being together like it is in the
movies and in the popular songs of the forties where it's all
lovely and there are no troubles connected with it. This is
not an unworthy ideal, nor is it contemptible. It can result
in some bad human situations and has, doubtless, many times,
and will again. But if you are willing to pay the price of
anxiety and possible disgrace, an adulterous situation is frequently, for a very short period of time, absolutely glorious.
It's everything that you never had in your marriage, or never

since the very beginning of it. There is a paradox in tionship between men and women: the more used to they are, the less exciting they are to each othe a terrible thing. If there were any justice in the world, things wouldn't be that way. But there *isn't* any justice in the world in that sense, and things *are* that way.

I think, for example, that for a man to see a relative stranger naked is the ultimate for him, until just after he's done it. But to see somebody naked he's seen naked a thousand times is not exciting. Although he would die for her, she is not exciting to him. All of these factors enter into an adulterous relationship. It's no good saying that a person ought not to feel this way; it's very obvious that he *does* feel this way. He is willing to risk a very perilous and terrifying situation; he will risk *everything* for a bit of intensity that he thought he would never have again. It's not just weak and callow people who do this. It is the most imaginative and vital people who are going to be drawn to adultery. People who are quite willing to give up and give in to conventionality and the *status quo* are not going to be tempted by an adulterous possibility as much as people in whom the life instinct and sense of adventure is extremely strong. I don't mean to hold a little *Playboy* forum on adultery, but it was out of such considerations that I wrote "Adultery" in which the man says at the end that what he is doing is not totally bad, because "Guilt is magical."

It *is* magical. Baudelaire says somewhere that most sexual excitement comes from the knowledge of doing wrong. When we have complete social permissiveness, we're going to lose quite a lot of the sexual turn-on we're capable of. When we are no longer forbidden beings to each other, fallen from Grace, but simply pieces of meat, that's not going to be good for us. I want very much to cling to a remnant of the Puritan Ethic, even though I've written against it in poems like "May Day Sermon." But in a poem like "Adultery" I just turn around and say that maybe guilt is a terrific sexual stimulus, which it damned well is! I remember how exciting it was for me to kiss a girl in high school, because I knew I wasn't supposed to. And when I got her dress up her legs a little way, that was "gangbusters"! That was terrific; nothing could be more marvelous. Nowadays I'm fighting very hard, as I think everybody else ought to be fighting, against the notion of sex as mere meat. I don't believe in killing off the mystery of it. And part of the mystery is in flying in the face of the previous or current ethical tradition. It was out of notions such as these that the poem "Adultery" was written.

"Encounter in the Cage Country" is a zoo poem. All poets write zoo poems. This was mine. In London a few years ago on a halfway decent afternoon my family and I wanted to get out and do something in the open air, since it wasn't raining *that* day. They wanted to see historic monuments around London. But I have never liked monuments since the time we returned from our first visit to Europe, and I went to see *La Dolce Vita*. I thought to myself, "My God, Jim! Is this the kind of thing that goes on in Rome while you've been walking around looking at monuments?" I've mistrusted them ever since. But my family wanted to see monuments, so I sent them off. I went to a pub and started drinking and talking to whoever came in. I left the pub in the middle of the afternoon. I had a check from *The New Yorker* or *The Atlantic* in my pocket, and I got the "buying fever." I just wanted to buy something: anything! Well, I went into a surplus house and bought a pair of American dark glasses, the California type. I started walking around London, and I thought maybe someone would mistake me for Marcello Mastroianni. I'd been drinking for five hours, or I'd've had no such illusions!

Finally I found myself at the London Zoo and I thought, "Well, Jim, why not? You write about animals; maybe you ought to go in and have a look at a few *real* ones!" So I looked at the ostriches, elephants and rhinoceroses. But I really like predatory birds and animals, so I went over to the hawks and eagles. Finally I went into the cat house, or perhaps I should say the "feline enclosure." I walked over to the lion's cage and tried to relate to him. But he wouldn't give me the time of day. So I walked down past the ocelots, jaguars, and tigers, until I came to the black leopard's cage. And there it was, because he dropped the meat he was chewing and came over to the edge of the cage as though to say to me, "Where have you been? Did you bring it?" Maybe I did bring it, I don't know! To this day I don't know what he saw in me, whether it was my dark glasses, the way I dressed, the fact that I was an American, or my *soul*. But it was instant recognition on his part. He was terribly interested and very patient with me. I walked up and down in front of his cage and he went right along with me. I made as if to run, and he bounded down to the end of his cage as though not to let me get away. So "Encounter in the Cage Country" is about one of those recognition situations where one of the parties, in this case a caged animal in the zoo, knows what the recognition is and the other, in this case a poet, has yet to find out what it is. He has to ponder it, maybe for the rest of his life.

"For the Last Wolverine" is about extinction. I've always been particularly horrified of extinction. I don't mind dying myself, but I don't want to become extinct. I'm always looking at wildlife magazines to see what species are in danger of extinction. I tend to identify with animals. I identify with the shark. I don't know why; it's a very unlovely beast. But I also identify with the wolverine. I can understand that identification a little better, because to me the wolverine is the ultimate wild animal. Very few people, even those who live in Alaska, have ever seen one. But they're legendarily canny, wild, savage, shrewd, diabolical, and rare. When I found out that the wolverine was in danger of becoming extinct, it hit me like a terrifying blow, because I like to think that when that kind of ultimate wildness dies out, something goes in man, too. There's a rough parallel to this in Romain Gary's book, *The Roots of Heaven*, about a man who dedicated his life to preventing the extinction of the elephant. Think, for example, that there would never be another elephant, not even one! Because when the last one dies—the last two—the possibility of reproducing the species dies. They would be gone with the dodo, the quagga, the passenger pigeon, and the heath hen. Even now the American bison, whooping crane, California condor, and American eagle are in danger of extinction. So is the wolverine.

When I wrote this poem I thought that maybe two nearly extinct species that never had anything to do with each other would be given special powers because they were near extinction. The last wolverine and the last eagle might then mate in the top of a big tree and raise up a phoenix-like, avenging creature, a wolverine that could fly. It would be a crafty, diabolical creature, possessed of an ultimate savagery, that would be immortal and would terrorize all the people who tried to industrialize or civilize the North Woods country. At the end of the poem the poet realizes that this is just a fantasy. The last wolverine will be crouching under a bush, a filthy little animal that nobody gives a damn about. But the poet, a man who believes in the wildness, savagery, and mystery of the wolverine, invokes the spirit of the wolverine to enter the poems he will write in the future. And in what is an oblique commentary on the possible extinction of the human race, he reconciles himself to his own death but asks the god of the universe or the god of the wildness of poetry, not to let his kind die out:

> *Lord, let me die   but not die*
> *Out.*

"The Bee" is a tribute to old football coaches. Among intellectuals I realize that football players are looked on as proto-fascist figures. But I have never had anything but the most extreme gratitude for my football coaches. In retrospect, the bad times they gave me come to seem like acts of faith, because they wouldn't have taken the time with me if they didn't think I was worth it. It was hard at the time to realize this, though.

This poem is based largely on an incident concerning myself and my youngest son, Kevin. We were going out to an archery range—Kevin loved to walk in the woods with me when I shot arrows—and were getting out of the car by the highway when a bee came out of the woods and stung him. In his panic he stumbled out onto the California highway where the cars were going by at eighty miles an hour. In the poem the father—sometimes I speak of the poet or the protagonist, but in this case it really was me—calls on his last physical resources to reach the boy and trip him up before he can get himself killed. What the father calls on is the last residue of energy that his old coaches gave him twenty-five years ago by continually abusing him in such terms as "get the lead out," "get off a dime," and many others not mentionable here. And he does barely, barely save his son. They are both scratched from falling on the edge of the highway, where the cars go by without anybody noticing anything unusual, and they go off into the woods pretty badly shaken. The little boy, exhausted from his terror, lies down in his father's arms under a tree, as the father silently thinks of his old coaches, long dead, who have given him the physical power and the quick start to get to the little boy and save him. As the father says, "Dead coaches live in the air . . ." and they keep urging him on, because they want him to be better than he is. Again, the act of the coaches riding him all the time is actually an announcement of their belief that he's capable of doing more than he thought he could.

"The Leap" was written about an actual situation, a memory. I knew a girl who was a fast runner in the seventh grade when the boys and girls used to run relay races against each other. I also have one brief flash in my mind of the same girl coming into a school dance and jumping up to touch the decorations. She was a very athletic little girl. I don't believe I ever saw her since that time, but I saw a picture of her in an Atlanta paper, a mother of four, and she had jumped out of a hotel window. In this poem I tried to ponder the relationship of her tomboyism in grade school, the athletic action of jumping to touch the decorations at the dance when she was committed to becoming a woman instead of a tomboy, and the results of her being a woman. She married a man whom she didn't get along with, had his children, and eventually committed suicide because of it. This was yet one more leap, this time the final one from the window of a hotel. The protagonist in the poem looks at the newspaper and doesn't believe that the suicide really happened. But he remembers these incidents and concludes that for some inexplicable reason it did happen. The images come together in his mind.

"Coming Back to America" has to do with the American experience. We live in a land of enormously high buildings and tremendous efficiency and dissipation. The poem is about an American family who come back from Europe to New York City and drive down from the ship in their automobile to the basement parking lot of an American high-rise hotel. They get the full traumatic effect of coming back to their own country with all its efficiency and indifference. They can get ice cubes in the hall of their hotel, and they feel they must get drunk immediately to celebrate, or to exorcise Europe and welcome the American experience again. They drink madly in this alien environment which is really their home environment. Very early the next morning the man wakes up with a terrible hangover, and goes up for a swim to the pool on the roof. There's nobody there but a girl lifeguard with a terribly scarred leg. They talk a bit, and he falls into a fantasy about her while watching her swim in the pool at dawn.

The greatest thing your own country can do for you is perpetually to be able to surprise you. You expect foreign countries to surprise you, but the greatest thing your own country can do for you is to do something unexpected to you or for you. The man feels that this skinny girl with the Brooklyn accent swimming alone at dawn in the pool of an enormous high-rise hotel is sort of the goddess-figure of the perpetually unknowable about his own country.

"False Youth" is in two parts. I was originally going to write four seasons, but I only wrote two seasons, winter and summer. In these poems the writing problem that interested me had to do with the times when one has the illusion that time has not passed, that one is still seventeen. I believe that I'm seventeen. I don't believe that I'm forty-six, *really*. Seventeen actually seems to be my age. I don't buy what Yeats says about age bringing wisdom. I don't really believe that my body will ever fail, that I'll go blind, my heart will stop, and I'll die, because I'm really seventeen. Whenever I stop and think, I know what I am, and my body surely tells me what I am, but *really* I feel that I'm seventeen. These two poems are about the kind of feeling you occasionally have, unfortunately less and less. Sometimes you feel a sense of absolute assurance and power in middle age which is characteristic only of youth, so it's a kind of false youth. These are two poems about incidents in which this sense of false youth occurs.

The first part, about summer, is about a man who has been recalled into military service. He's dating a girl who works a computer at the air base where he's stationed, and he's married with children practically her age. They're sitting in the South on a porch swing like young lovers, and he has a momentary feeling that he really *is* a young lover. They're holding hands and she's telling him how she works the computer at the base. And although he's fat and middle-aged, he has this momentary feeling that she's with him for no other reason than that he's a young man her age courting her on the swing. God knows, this happens! It does, and it should.

The second part is about a teacher—maybe the same man as on the porch swing, but probably not—who takes his student home in an ice storm and delivers her there safely. He's invited into the house and talks to her blind grandmother. There's a tradition in the South that what a blind person tells you is true: that a blind person can feel your face and tell you not only what you look like but what your character is like. All my life I've heard that you can't fool blind people. The grandmother feels the teacher's face—he's about thirty-nine or forty years old—and says, "My God, to have a growing boy." He's not going to fly in the face of Providence and answer, "Oh no, ma'am, you may be blind, but you're wrong!" He accepts it, not to save her feelings, but because he's quite happy to have this kind of confirmation that he really isn't aging. Then he leaves, determined to seek out the blind wherever they may be found, and abide by their wisdom.

I suppose if any poem of mine has gotten much attention, "Falling" has. The original idea came out of a newspaper item I once read to the effect that an Allegheny Airlines stewardess had fallen out of an airplane and was found later on, dead. But when you have a little hint like this that entertains your imagination, you take off with it and make your own thing out of it. I made her fall from an airplane over the Midwest. It's not a jet. People think of it as a jet, but it couldn't possibly be a jet. If it had been a jet, it would be so high that she would have been flash-frozen. But if you're a poet, you can make it happen the way you want it to. So I made the plane one that would be flying at a speed and altitude over the Midwest at which such a thing could happen to the stewardess.

"Falling" is a record of the way she feels as she falls: panic at first and then a kind of goddess-like invulnerability. She discovers that the human body can actually fly a little bit. She tries to find water to fall into, but in the end she can't and falls into a cornfield and dies there. She undresses on the way down, because since she's going to die she wants to die, as she says, "beyond explanation." She would rather be found naked in a cornfield than in an airline uniform. So she takes off everything, is clean, purely desirable, purely woman, and dies in that way. I also tried to think of the mystical possibility there might be for farmers in that vicinity, under those conditions.

Many different interpretations have been given to this poem. A lot of people say that it's too far-fetched, that nothing like this would really happen. I'm quite sure it wouldn't. But I was interested in trying to determine, by using my own particular capacities, what *might* conceivably go on. I was interested in using the kind of time-telescoping effect that Bergson talks about in discussing the difference between clock time and lived time. It takes twenty minutes to read the poem, more or less. It surely wouldn't have taken her nearly that long to fall. But as to how long it *seemed* to her, that's quite a different thing. Time has a way of widening out when you're in an extreme adrenalin kind of situation. I felt justified in writing "Falling" the way I did. I wouldn't want to go back and try to write it again. I suppose there are faults in it which people will be pointing out to me for years, but I did it the way I wanted to do it, and I'll stand by that.

FALLING

> *A 29-year-old stewardess fell . . . to her*
> *death tonight when she was swept*
> *through an emergency door that sud-*
> *denly sprang open . . . The body . . .*
> *was found . . . three hours after the*
> *accident.*
>
> —*New York Times*

The states when they black out and lie there rolling   when they turn
To something transcontinental   move by   drawing moonlight out
    of the great
One-sided stone hung off the starboard wingtip   some sleeper next to
An engine is groaning for coffee   and there is faintly coming in
Somewhere the vast beast-whistle of space. In the galley with its racks
Of trays   she rummages for a blanket   and moves in her slim
    tailored
Uniform to pin it over the cry at the top of the door. As though she blew

The door down with a silent blast from her lungs   frozen   she is
    black
Out finding herself   with the plane nowhere and her body taking by
    the throat
The undying cry of the void   falling   living   beginning to be
    something
That no one has ever been and lived through   screaming without
    enough air
Still neat   lipsticked   stockinged   girdled by regulation   her
    hat
Still on   her arms and legs in no world   and yet spaced also
    strangely
With utter placid rightness on thin air   taking her time   she holds
    it
In many places   and now, still thousands of feet from her death
    she seems
To slow   she develops interest   she turns in her maneuverable body

To watch it. She is hung high up in the overwhelming middle of things in her

Self   in low body-whistling wrapped intensely   in all her dark dance-weight

Coming down from a marvellous leap   with the delaying, dumfounding ease

Of a dream of being drawn   like endless moonlight to the harvest soil

Of a central state of one's country   with a great gradual warmth coming

Over her   floating   finding more and more breath in what she has been using

For breath   as the levels become more human   seeing clouds placed honestly

Below her left and right   riding slowly toward them   she clasps it all

To her and can hang her hands and feet in it in peculiar ways   and

Her eyes opened wide by wind, can open her mouth as wide   wider and suck

All the heat from the cornfields   can go down on her back with a feeling

Of stupendous pillows stacked under her   and can turn   turn as to someone

In bed   smile, understood in darkness   can go away   slant slide

Off tumbling   into the emblem of a bird with its wings half-spread

Or whirl madly on herself   in endless gymnastics in the growing warmth

Of wheatfields rising toward the harvest moon.   There is time to live

In superhuman health   seeing mortal unreachable lights far down seeing

An ultimate highway with one late priceless car probing it   arriving

In a square town   and off her starboard arm the glitter of water catches

The moon by its one shaken side   scaled, roaming silver   My God it is good

And evil   lying in one after another of all the positions for love

Making   dancing   sleeping   and now cloud wisps at her no

Raincoat   no matter   all small towns brokenly brighter from inside

Cloud   she walks over them like rain   bursts out to behold a
     Greyhound
Bus shooting light through its sides   it is the signal to go straight
Down like a glorious diver   then feet first   her skirt stripped
     beautifully
Up   her face in fear-scented cloths   her legs deliriously bare
     then
Arms out   she slow-rolls over   steadies out   waits for something
     great
To take control of her   trembles near feathers   planes head-down
The quick movements of bird-necks turning her head   gold eyes
     the insight-
eyesight of owls blazing into the hencoops   a taste for chicken
     overwhelming
Her   the long-range vision of hawks enlarging all human lights
     of cars
Freight trains   looped bridges   enlarging the moon racing slowly
Through all the curves of a river   all the darks of the midwest blazing
From above. A rabbit in a bush turns white   the smothering chickens
Huddle   for over them there is still time for something to live
With the streaming half-idea of a long stoop   a hurtling   a fall
That is controlled   that plummets as it wills   turns gravity
Into a new condition, showing its other side like a moon   shining
New Powers   there is still time to live on a breath made of nothing
But the whole night   time for her to remember to arrange her skirt
Like a diagram of a bat   tightly it guides her   she has this
     flying-skin
Made of garments   and there are also those sky-divers on TV
     sailing
In sunlight   smiling under their goggles   swapping batons back
     and forth
And He who jumped without a chute and was handed one by a diving
Buddy. She looks for her grinning companion   white teeth
     nowhere
She is screaming   singing hymns   her thin human wings spread out
From her neat shoulders   the air beast-crooning to her   warbling

And she can no longer behold the huge partial form of the world   now
She is watching her country lose its evoked master shape   watching
    it lose
And gain   get back its houses and peoples   watching it bring up
Its local lights   single homes   lamps on barn roofs   if she fell
Into water she might live   like a diver   cleaving   perfect
    plunge

Into another   heavy silver   unbreathable   slowing   saving
Element: there is water   there is time to perfect all the fine
Points of diving   feet together   toes pointed   hands shaped right
To insert her into water like a needle   to come out healthily dripping
And be handed a Coca-Cola   there they are   there are the waters
Of life   the moon packed and coiled in a reservoir   so let me begin
To plane across the night air of Kansas   opening my eyes
    superhumanly
Bright   to the dammed moon   opening the natural wings of my jacket
By Don Loper   moving like a hunting owl toward the glitter of water
One cannot just fall   just tumble screaming all that time   one must
    use
It   she is now through with all   through all   clouds   damp
    hair
Straightened   the last wisp of fog pulled apart on her face like wool
    revealing
New darks   new progressions of headlights along dirt roads
    from chaos

And night   a gradual warming   a new-made, inevitable world of
    one's own
Country   a great stone of light in its waiting waters   hold   hold
    out
For water: who knows when what correct young woman must take up
    her body
And fly   and head for the moon-crazed inner eye of midwest
    imprisoned
Water   stored up for her for years   the arms of her jacket slipping
Air up her sleeves to go   all over her? What final things can be said

Of one who starts out sheerly in her body in the high middle of night
Air   to track down water like a rabbit where it lies like life itself
Off to the right in Kansas? She goes toward   the blazing-bare lake
Her skirts neat   her hands and face warmed more and more by the air
Rising from pastures of beans   and under her   under chenille
    bedspreads
The farm girls are feeling the goddess in them struggle and rise
    brooding
On the scratch-shining posts of the bed   dreaming of female signs
Of the moon   male blood like iron   of what is really said by the moan
Of airliners passing over them at dead of midwest midnight   passing
Over brush fires   burning out in silence on little hills   and will wake
To see the woman they should be   struggling on the rooftree to become
Stars: for her the ground is closer   water is nearer   she passes
It   then banks   turns   her sleeves fluttering differently as she rolls
Out to face the east, where the sun shall come up from wheatfields
    she must
Do something with water   fly to it   fall in it   drink it   rise
From it   but there is none left upon earth   the clouds have drunk
    it back
The plants have sucked it down   there are standing toward her only
The common fields of death   she comes back from flying to falling
Returns to a powerful cry   the silent scream with which she blew down
The coupled door of the airliner   nearly   nearly losing hold
Of what she has done   remembers   remembers the shape at the
    heart
Of cloud   fashionably swirling   remembers she still has time to die
Beyond explanation. Let her now take off her hat in summer air the
    contour
Of cornfields   and have enough time to kick off her one remaining
Shoe with the toes   of the other foot   to unhook her stockings
With calm fingers, noting how fatally easy it is to undress in midair
Near death   when the body will assume without effort any position
Except the one that will sustain it   enable it to rise   live
Not die   nine farms hover close   widen   eight of them separate,
    leaving

One in the middle   then the fields of that farm do the same   there
    is no
Way to back off   from her chosen ground   but she sheds the jacket
With its silver sad impotent wings   sheds the bat's guiding tailpiece
Of her skirt   the lightning-charged clinging of her blouse   the
    intimate
Inner flying-garment of her slip in which she rides like the holy ghost
Of a virgin   sheds the long windsocks of her stockings   absurd
Brassiere   then feels the girdle required by regulations squirming
Off her: no longer monobuttocked   she feels the girdle flutter
    shake
In her hand   and float   upward   her clothes rising off her
    ascending
Into cloud   and fights away from her head the last sharp dangerous
    shoe
Like a dumb bird   and now will drop in   SOON   now will drop

In like this   the greatest thing that ever came to Kansas   down
    from all
Heights   all levels of American breath   layered in the lungs
    from the frail
Chill of space to the loam where extinction slumbers in corn tassels
    thickly
And breathes like rich farmers counting: will come among them after
Her last superhuman act   the last slow careful passing of her hands
All over her unharmed body   desired by every sleeper in his dream:
Boys finding for the first time their loins filled with heart's blood
Widowed farmers whose hands float under light covers to find
    themselves
Arisen at sunrise   the splendid position of blood unearthly drawn
Toward clouds   all feel something   pass over them as she passes
Her palms over *her* long legs   *her* small breasts   and deeply between
Her thighs   her hair shot loose from all pins   streaming in the wind
Of her body   let her come openly   trying at the last second to land
On her back   This is it   THIS

                       All those who find her impressed
In the soft loam   gone down   driven well into the image of her body

The furrows for miles flowing in upon her where she lies very deep
In her mortal outline   in the earth as it is in cloud   can tell nothing
But that she is there   inexplicable   unquestionable   and
     remember
That something broke in them as well   and began to live and die more
When they walked for no reason into their fields to where the whole
     earth
Caught her   interrupted her maiden flight   told her how to lie
     she cannot
Turn   go away   cannot move   cannot slide off it and assume
     another
Position   no sky-diver with any grin could save her   hold her in
     his arms
Plummet with her   unfold above her his wedding silks   she can no
     longer
Mark the rain with whirling women that take the place of a dead wife
Or the goddess in Norwegian farm girls   or all the back-breaking
     whores
Of Wichita. All the known air above her is not giving up quite one
Breath   it is all gone   and yet not dead   not anywhere else
Quite   lying still in the field on her back   sensing the smells
Of incessant growth try to lift her   a little sight left in the corner
Of one eye   fading   seeing something wave   lies believing
That she could have made it   at the best part of her brief goddess
State   to water   gone in headfirst   come out smiling
     invulnerable
Girl in a bathing-suit ad   but she is lying like a sunbather at the last
Of moonlight   half-buried in her impact on the earth   not far
From a railroad trestle   a water tank   she could see if she could
Raise her head from her modest hole   with her clothes beginning
To come down all over Kansas   into bushes   on the dewy sixth green
Of a golf course   one shoe   her girdle coming down fantastically
On a clothesline, where it belongs   her blouse on a lightning rod:

Lies in the fields   in *this* field   on her broken back as though on
A cloud she cannot drop through   while farmers sleepwalk without
Their women from houses   a walk like falling toward the far waters

Of life   in moonlight   toward the dreamed eternal meaning of
    their farms
Toward the flowering of the harvest in their hands   that tragic cost
Feels herself go   go toward   go outward   breathes at last fully
Not   and tries   less   once   tries   tries   AH, GOD—

The poem, "May Day Sermon," came in some manner from a statement by Edwin Arlington Robinson, which I read years ago in a collection of his letters. The quotation, as I remember it, says that, I have been reading the Old Testament as though it were a novel, and I am convinced that God is the villain. It hit me that God, whether by nature a villain or a hero, can be *made* a villain by villainous people. I am not sure whether or not the Old Testament shows this, as Robinson thinks it does, but I have seen a good deal of evidence for this supposition in events in my own life. "May Day Sermon" is about that, and about the malevolent power God has under certain circumstances: that is, when He is controlled and "interpreted" by people of malevolent tendencies. In this case God is neither more nor less than a combination of the Old Testament and a half-mad Georgia hill farmer. The natural inclinations of his daughter, particularly in the spring of the year, are interpreted by him as "sin," and he drags her into the barn, strips her, and beats her nearly to death. What I wanted to do most in this poem was to make a kind of mythological framework for the action by casting the poem in the form of one of the legends that are prevalent in such communities. The ghost story, the house which everyone avoids because of what happened there years ago, the land that surrounded such a place, and the absorption of these details into the minds of a community, are what the poem is about. It has, I like to think, something to do with the ingrained attitude of mythologizing that rural communities have. What originated as a story of rural blood lust and religion and sex and escape has now become something of a legend, and the woman preacher who speaks the poem has taken that legend as her text, and also as her valedictory to the Baptist church, which is in some manner connected with the events of the legend. I have always liked local stories and reminiscences and legends, and it seemed to me that in the telling of this one there were a good many elements which are present in, and a good many elements which are absent from most of the legends that we hear. I wanted to make the Bible, or a certain interpretation of the Bible which permits cruelty, the final focus of the poem. I also wanted to connect what happens to the people in the poem with the animals—in this case those in the barn—of the world. I wanted to do what I have for many years attempted to do: that is make a long, long poem which has a kind of unbridled frenzy about it, something like that frenzy found when a preacher—particularly of the rural, Baptist variety—works himself up into a state of fanatical, Biblical, unbridled frenzy "as though he were pure spirit, beyond good and evil." I like to think that readers will notice the parallel between the frenzy on the part of the father—a kind of frenzy of cruelty and self-righteousness—and the frenzy of the woman preacher, who is convinced she is right in telling the women of Gilmer County to throw off the shackles of the Baptist religion and enter into an older world of springtime, pleasure, love and delight. Various readers and critics have made various things of the poem, but it really is a very simple one. It is just a retelling of a local folk myth.

Concerning the future, I want to write one more book which uses some split line techniques. I evolved the split line to try to do what I could to reproduce as nearly as I could the real way of the mind as it associates verbally. The mind doesn't seem to work in a straight line, but associates in bursts of words, in jumps. I used this technique for "Falling" in a more pronounced form and wrote such poems as "Slave Quarters" and "The Firebombing" in a more modified form. I want to write a few more poems using these or different modifications of the technique. But I think I'll be moving more and more toward a narrative with less direct continuity than I've had before. I expect that this will inevitably result in my becoming more obscure than I have been. I want to work with extremely crazy, apparently unjustifiable juxtapositions and sudden shifts of meaning or consciousness. I have always believed in the principle of uncertainty—not exactly Heisenberg's Indeterminacy Principle in physics—but in something similar in human affairs. The poet tries to make a kind of order, or as somebody said— maybe it was Robert Frost—a momentary stay against confusion. But you have to realize that in the last analysis, it's actually the order of art only. Art must have this order; it would not be possible except for the divine *dis*order of human experience. Maybe there will come a poetry which, through a kind of supernal order, will show the chance factor in human affairs and will be able to reproduce, through its own means, the effect of the disorder of human existence. This poetry will in the end have to be orderly but seem to be disorderly. If what I wish to do works out, I'll write even more discontinuous and undoubtedly more obscure poems, moving, I hope, eventually toward a greater clarity than I or anybody else has yet had. We can hope. Indeed, we must, and sometimes we can.

"In the Tree House at Night,"
111–12
Into the Stone, 45, 46, 48, 83,
84, 91, 99, 123
"Into the Stone," 98–99

James, Henry, 52, 61
James, William, 124
Jarrell, Randall, 34, 85
Jeffers, Robinson, 77
Jerome, Judson, 70
Johnson, Lyndon Baines, 31
John the Baptist, 143
Jonson, Ben, 16

Kazantzakis, Nikos, 76
Keats, John, 16, 74–76, 119
Kennedy, John F., 71
Kennedy, Robert, 70

Lalley, James, 93, 114–15
Lawrence, D. H., 55, 67
"Leap, The," 172
Leary, Paris, 99
Leege, Gwendolyn, 26
Leigh, Augusta, 23
Leviton, Jay, 132
"Lifeguard, The," 101–5
"Listening to Foxhounds," 105
Longfellow, Henry Wadsworth,
25
Longinus, Dionysius, 65
Lowry, Malcolm, 24, 74, 76
Lytle, Andrew, 33, 42, 43

MacDonald, Dwight, 31
McKillop, Alan D., 42
Malinowski, Bronislaw, 36
Malraux, André, 135
"Mangham," 152
Marvell, Andrew, 71
Masson, Loys, 112

Mastroianni, Marcello, 168
"May Day Sermon," 167, 183–
84
Merrill, James, 131
Michelangelo Buonarroti, 133
Millay, Edna St. Vincent, 53
Milton, John, 27, 54
Montherlant, Henry de, 60
Moore, Marianne, 106
Moss, Howard, 84

Nemerov, Howard, 31
"Night Pool, The," 148–49

"On a Hill Below the Lighthouse," 85, 87, 98
"Owl King, The," 112–14

Palmer, John, 40
Parmenides, 55–56
Pascal, Blaise, 37
Patchen, Kenneth, 27, 29
"Performance, The," 91, 92–96
Picasso, Pablo, 32
Plath, Sylvia, 137
Plato, 131
Poe, Edgar Allan, 12
Poems 1957–1967, 9, 15, 49
"Poisoned Man, The," 131–32
Pound, Ezra, 47
Prentice, Sargent, 26
Price, Cecil, 140

Radcliffe-Brown, Alfred, 36
Rainey, Lawrence A., 141
Ransom, John Crowe, 33
"Reincarnation (I)," 140–41
"Reincarnation (II)," 60, 140,
163
Richards, I. A., 52
Riesman, David, 92, 154

I am Blue
1623